M000311422

Fresh Fields

For Allan
who encouraged me
and had faith in my talent
and love for cooking

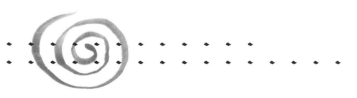

FreshFields

A CELEBRATION OF GOOD FOOD

by
Sherron Goldstein

Art by Jill Fineberg

This cookbook is a collection of favorite recipes, which
are not necessarily all original recipes.

Copyright© Sherron Goldstein
3809 Crestside Road
Birmingham, Alabama 35223

All rights reserved. No part of this book may be reproduced or transmitted
in any form or by any means, electronic or mechanical, including photocopying,
recording, or by any information storage and retrieval system, without
prior written permission from the publisher.

Library of Congress Catalog Number: 98-092726
ISBN: 0-9663343-0-2

Designed and Manufactured by
Favorite Recipes® Press
an imprint of

FRP

P.O. Box 305142, Nashville, Tennessee 37230
800-358-0560

Project Manager: Debbie Van Mol
Book Design: Janet Brooks
Art Director: Steve Newman
Project Production: Sara Anglin

Manufactured in the United States of America
First Printing: 1998   4,000 copies

CONTENTS

Introduction • 6

INTRODUCTION

I grew up in a household where food was a presentation of love. I could label my mother's cooking as "foods of comfort": fresh, seasonal, and always satisfying.

Some of my warmest memories are of my mother and my sister-in-law Pat, preparing large family feasts that filled their homes with delicious aromas, always promising a potpourri of wonderful tastes. We all came to the dinner table feeling the warm sharing of good food, love, and flavorful memories. It is these early influences that created the comfort and pleasure I feel in the kitchen.

Cooking is a creative art. Food is about nourishment and fueling the body. Combining the two reveals an opportunity to create healthier and more nutritious choices for ourselves. By using the freshest seasonal ingredients available, enhanced with flavorful herbs and spices, we can create enticing foods with dynamic tastes.

Naively, this book began as a collection of recipes: my personal history uniquely blended with family favorites, and some shared by friends that appreciate my passion for cooking. The original intent was to pass these recipes on to my three daughters, Stefanie, Melissa, and Jennifer, that they might, as many families do, feed and nourish themselves with conversation, nurturing food, and memorable gatherings as has happened so often in our own kitchen at home. What resulted is a presentation of food preparation that expresses my personal desire for creating fresh foods, with uncomplicated, honest flavors.

My hope is that this cookbook will be an inspiration to cook at home. Food does not have to be complicated to be good. Prepared with thoughtfulness, and lovingly served, food will fuel the body and fill the spirit.

ENJOY!

Sherron Goldstein

Appetizers

Jack Daniel's Spiced Pecans

Serves 6

butter or margarine

¹/₂ cup sugar

¹/₄ cup Jack Daniel's
No. 7 Whiskey or
2 tablespoons water

1 teaspoon salt

1 teaspoon chili powder

³/₄ teaspoon cayenne

2 cups pecan halves

- ◆ Line a baking sheet with foil and coat with butter.

- ◆ Combine the sugar, whiskey, salt, chili powder and cayenne in a saucepan.

- ◆ Cook over medium heat until the sugar dissolves, stirring frequently. Bring to a boil.

- ◆ Boil gently for 3 minutes, stirring occasionally.

- ◆ Add the pecans, stirring until coated. Spread the pecans in a single layer on the prepared baking sheet.

- ◆ Bake at 250 degrees for 15 to 20 minutes.

- ◆ Let stand until cool.

Hot Spinach Dip in Pumpernickel

Serves 10 to 12

2 (10-ounce) packages frozen chopped spinach, thawed

¹/2 cup chopped green onions

¹/2 cup packed chopped fresh parsley

2 tablespoons chopped garlic

¹/4 cup margarine

3 tablespoons flour

1 cup light sour cream

1 tablespoon Worcestershire sauce

1 teaspoon freshly ground pepper

8 ounces grated Parmesan cheese

1 large round loaf pumpernickel bread

◆ Squeeze the moisture from the spinach, reserving ¹/2 cup of the liquid.

◆ Sauté the green onions, parsley and garlic in the margarine in a saucepan until tender. Stir in the flour.

◆ Sauté for 1 minute. Add the reserved liquid, sour cream, Worcestershire sauce and pepper gradually and mix well.

◆ Cook until thickened, stirring constantly. Add the cheese.

◆ Cook until the cheese melts, stirring constantly. Remove from heat. Fold in the spinach.

◆ Hollow out the bread loaf carefully, leaving a ¹/2-inch shell. Spoon the spinach dip into the shell.

◆ Serve with assorted party crackers or freshly cut vegetables.

Note:
Substitute a head of purple cabbage or cauliflower for the loaf of bread for variety.

 Tomato Corn Salsa   Serves 12

6 large tomatoes, chopped

2 cups fresh corn, blanched

1 cup chopped red onion

1 cup garbanzo beans

1/2 cup chopped fresh cilantro

4 Anaheim chiles, chopped

6 green onions, chopped

6 cloves of garlic, chopped

Juice of 1 lime

1 tablespoon hot sauce

1 teaspoon freshly ground
    pepper

- ◆ Combine the tomatoes, corn, onion, garbanzo beans, cilantro, chiles, green onions, garlic, lime juice, hot sauce and pepper in a bowl and mix well.

- ◆ Serve with assorted chips.

 Baba Ghanouj   Serves 12

1 medium eggplant

1 recipe Hummus bi Tahini
    (page 15)

fresh lemon juice

chopped fresh parsley

pita bread

- ◆ Pierce the eggplant with a fork. Place in a baking pan.

- ◆ Broil until tender, turning frequently. Let stand until cool.

- ◆ Peel the eggplant and mash. Combine the eggplant with the hummus in a bowl and mix well.

- ◆ Add cold water, stirring until thickened. Add lemon juice, stirring until of the desired consistency.

- ◆ Spoon into a serving bowl. Sprinkle with parsley.

- ◆ Serve with pita bread.

Note:
Add additional garlic if desired.

Black Olive and Feta Bruschetta

Serves 6 to 8

1 baguette French bread

extra-virgin olive oil

1/2 red or yellow bell pepper, roasted, chopped

1/2 cup crumbled feta cheese

1/2 cup chopped kalamata olives

1/4 cup chopped fresh parsley

2 cloves of garlic, finely chopped

1 teaspoon lemon juice

freshly cracked pepper to taste

◆ Cut the bread into 1/2-inch slices. Brush both sides generously with olive oil.

◆ Arrange the bread slices in a single layer on a nonstick baking sheet.

◆ Bake at 400 degrees until golden brown. Let stand until cool.

◆ Combine the bell pepper, feta cheese, olives, parsley, garlic and lemon juice in a bowl and mix well. Season with pepper.

◆ Top each bread slice with a generous amount of the olive mixture.

◆ Arrange the bruschetta on a serving platter.

Ceviche with Avocado

Serves 8

1 pound firm white fish
1 cup fresh lemon juice
5 large tomatoes, peeled, seeded, chopped
1 large onion, chopped
12 pimento-stuffed green olives, chopped
1 yellow pepper, finely chopped
1/2 cup olive oil
2 tablespoons chopped fresh parsley
2 tablespoons chopped fresh cilantro
2 tablespoons chopped fresh thyme
2 medium avocados, chopped

- ◆ Cut the fish into bite-size pieces. Place in a bowl.
- ◆ Pour the lemon juice over the fish, turning to coat.
- ◆ Marinate, covered, in the refrigerator for 2 to 10 hours, stirring occasionally. Add the tomatoes, onion and olives and mix gently.
- ◆ Stir in the olive oil, parsley, cilantro and thyme.
- ◆ Chill, covered, for 4 to 6 hours. Stir in the avocado just before serving.
- ◆ Serve with assorted party crackers.

Pat's Crab Mold

Serves 10 to 12

1 envelope unflavored gelatin
1 to 2 tablespoons water
1 (10-ounce) can tomato soup
1/2 cup crab or clam juice
2 cups whipped light cream cheese
1/2 cup light mayonnaise
1/2 cup light sour cream
1 pound fresh crab meat
1 cup finely chopped celery
1/2 small onion, finely chopped

◆ Mix the gelatin and water in a bowl. Let stand until softened.

◆ Combine the tomato soup and crab juice in a saucepan.

◆ Cook until blended, stirring frequently.

◆ Add the gelatin mixture, stirring until mixed. Let stand until cool.

◆ Beat the cream cheese, mayonnaise and sour cream in a mixer bowl until smooth. Fold in the gelatin mixture. Stir in the crab meat, celery and onion.

◆ Spoon the crab mixture into a fish mold sprayed with nonstick cooking spray.

◆ Chill for 8 to 10 hours.

◆ Serve with rye rounds or other assorted party crackers.

 Garlic and Bean Crostini   Serves 6 to 8

1 loaf French bread

1 cup chicken or vegetable broth

1 cup canned cannellini beans

3 tablespoons cannellini bean liquid

1 tablespoon tomato purée

2 cloves of garlic, smashed, finely chopped

1 tablespoon rosemary, finely chopped

1/2 teaspoon red pepper flakes, finely chopped

3 tablespoons olive oil

Juice of 1 lemon

chopped fresh parsley

◆ Cut the bread into 1/2-inch slices. Arrange in a single layer on a nonstick baking sheet.

◆ Toast at 400 degrees for 3 to 5 minutes or until light brown on both sides, turning once.

◆ Heat the broth in a saucepan until lukewarm. Cover to keep warm.

◆ Process the beans and bean liquid in a food processor until puréed.

◆ Sauté the tomato purée, garlic, rosemary and red pepper flakes in the olive oil in a skillet for 2 minutes. Stir in the bean mixture and heated broth and mix well.

◆ Cook over medium heat for 10 minutes, stirring frequently; the mixture should be smooth. Stir in the lemon juice.

◆ Spread 1 heaping tablespoon of the bean mixture on each bread slice. Sprinkle with parsley.

◆ Arrange on a serving platter. Serve immediately.

 # Hummus

Serves 6

For the Tahini Sauce

1 cup tahini

6 tablespoons cold water

Juice of 3 lemons

4 cloves of garlic, crushed

$\frac{1}{2}$ teaspoon salt

For the Hummus

1 cup chick-peas

1 recipe Tahini Sauce

3 tablespoons olive oil

chopped fresh parsley or paprika

◆ To prepare the sauce, stir the tahini before measuring. Combine the tahini and cold water in a bowl and mix well.

◆ Add the lemon juice and stir until smooth.

◆ Mash the garlic with the salt in a bowl until it is the consistency of a paste. Stir into the sauce.

◆ To prepare the hummus, process the chick-peas in a food processor until smooth. Add the Tahini Sauce.

◆ Process until mixed. May add water if desired for a thinner consistency. Lemon juice may be added to cut the sesame flavor.

◆ Spoon the hummus into a serving dish with raised sides. Drizzle with the olive oil. Sprinkle with parsley or paprika.

Sun-Dried Tomato and Pesto Boursin Loaf

Serves 12

24 ounces cream cheese, softened

6 tablespoons butter or margarine, softened

4 large cloves of garlic, smashed, chopped

1 teaspoon dried thyme

1 teaspoon dried basil

1 teaspoon dried oregano

1 teaspoon dried dillweed

1 teaspoon dried marjoram

1 teaspoon salt-free seasoning mix

$^1/_3$ teaspoon freshly ground pepper

1 (3- to 4-ounce) jar pesto (basil, parsley, pine nuts and olive oil)

1 jar sun-dried tomatoes

◆ Drain the sun-dried tomatoes, pat dry and chop.

◆ Line a dish with plastic wrap, leaving enough plastic wrap overlapping to cover.

◆ Beat the cream cheese and butter in a mixer bowl until smooth, scraping the bowl occasionally. Add the garlic, thyme, basil, oregano, dillweed, marjoram and salt-free seasoning mix.

◆ Beat until blended.

◆ Chill, covered, for 15 minutes.

◆ Spread half the cream cheese mixture in the prepared dish. Spread evenly with the pesto.

◆ Sprinkle with $^1/_4$ cup of the sun-dried tomatoes. Spread with the remaining cream cheese mixture and smooth with a knife. Fold over the plastic wrap to cover.

◆ Chill for 4 hours or longer.

◆ Invert onto a serving tray; discard the plastic wrap. Sprinkle with the remaining sun-dried tomatoes.

◆ Serve with assorted party crackers.

Asparagus Cheese Toasts

Serves 4

4 ounces fresh asparagus,
trimmed

1 small onion, chopped

2 tablespoons butter or
margarine

1 cup shredded sharp Cheddar
cheese

1 tablespoon Grey Poupon
mustard (optional)

2 teaspoons Worcestershire
sauce

1 egg, beaten

freshly ground pepper to taste

6 slices bread, toasted

sliced cherry tomatoes

- ◆ Blanch the asparagus in a small amount of water in a saucepan for 3 minutes; drain. Let stand until cool

- ◆ Sauté the onion in the butter in a skillet until tender. Add the asparagus.

- ◆ Sauté for 2 minutes. Combine the asparagus mixture and cheese in a bowl and mix gently.

- ◆ Mix the mustard, Worcestershire sauce, egg and pepper in a bowl. Add to the asparagus mixture and mix well.

- ◆ Arrange the toasted bread in a single layer on a baking sheet lined with foil. Top each bread slice with some of the asparagus mixture.

- ◆ Bake at 350 degrees for 10 minutes.

- ◆ Cut each slice into 2 to 4 portions. Top each serving with a tomato slice.

Corn Pancakes with Smoked Trout and Caper Sauce

Serves 15 to 20

For the Caper Sauce

2 tablespoons white wine vinegar

2 egg yolks, beaten

1 tablespoon lemon juice

1 tablespoon Dijon mustard

1 tablespoon chopped garlic

1/4 teaspoon green peppercorns, crushed

1 cup olive oil

1 cup packed chopped fresh parsley

1/4 cup chopped fresh chives

1 (2-ounce) can anchovy fillets, drained, patted dry

2 teaspoons drained capers

For the Corn Pancakes

2/3 cup milk

2 tablespoons vegetable oil

1 egg

1 cup self-rising cornmeal

1 smoked trout fillet from the deli, flaked

chopped fresh parsley

- ◆ To prepare the sauce, heat the wine vinegar in a saucepan until simmering; do not boil.

- ◆ Combine the egg yolks, lemon juice, Dijon mustard, garlic and peppercorns in a food processor or blender container.

- ◆ Add the hot vinegar and olive oil in a fine stream, processing constantly until blended.

- ◆ Add the parsley, chives and anchovies.

- ◆ Process just until minced. Stir in the capers.

- ◆ To prepare the pancakes, whisk the milk, oil and egg in a bowl. Whisk in the cornmeal gradually; do not overmix.

- ◆ Pour just enough of the batter onto a hot lightly greased griddle to make pancakes the size of silver dollars.

- ◆ Cook until brown on both sides, turning once.

- ◆ Remove to a platter. Cover to keep warm.

- ◆ Repeat the process with the remaining batter.

- ◆ To assemble, arrange the warm pancakes on a serving platter.

- ◆ Top each pancake with a small portion of the smoked trout. Drizzle with the Caper Sauce and sprinkle with parsley.

 # Herbed Focaccia

Serves 8

1 pizza shell, baked
olive oil
1 tablespoon chopped garlic
¼ cup thinly sliced fresh basil
1 teaspoon dried thyme
1 teaspoon dried rosemary
½ cup sliced black or green
    olives
¼ cup grated Romano cheese
freshly ground pepper to taste

- ◆ Brush the pizza shell generously with olive oil.

- ◆ Sprinkle with the garlic, basil, thyme, rosemary and olives. Drizzle with olive oil.

- ◆ Sprinkle with the cheese and pepper.

- ◆ Bake at 425 degrees for 9 minutes.

Variation:

Sauté 1 large sliced onion in 1 tablespoon olive oil and spread over the pizza shell before sprinkling with the herbs for Onion Herb Focaccia.

 # Spinach Croustade

Serves 16

1 (10-ounce) package frozen chopped spinach

1/2 cup chopped onion

3 tablespoons butter or margarine

3 tablespoons flour

1/4 teaspoon dried marjoram

1/4 teaspoon dried rosemary

1/4 teaspoon dried mint

1/8 teaspoon pepper

1 cup evaporated skim milk

2 eggs, beaten or equivalent amount of egg substitute

1 cup creamy cottage cheese

1/2 cup crumbled feta cheese

10 sheets (about) frozen phyllo pastry, thawed

1/2 cup melted butter or margarine

◆ Cook the spinach using package directions; drain. Squeeze the moisture from the spinach.

◆ Sauté the onion in 3 tablespoons butter in a saucepan until tender. Stir in the flour, marjoram, rosemary, mint and pepper. Add the skim milk and mix well.

◆ Cook until thick and bubbly, stirring constantly.

◆ Stir half the hot mixture into the eggs. Return the mixture to the saucepan.

◆ Stir in the spinach, cottage cheese and feta cheese. Remove from heat.

◆ Place 1 sheet of the phyllo pastry on a work surface, leaving the remaining pastry covered with a damp towel to prevent drying out. Brush lightly with some of the 1/2 cup butter. Fold into thirds lengthwise and brush the top with butter.

◆ Place 1 end of the folded pastry in the center of a 12- or 14-inch-round baking pan, extending over the side of the pan.

◆ Repeat the process with the remaining pastry and arrange the strips evenly around the pan in a spoke fashion. (The ends of each sheet will overlap in the center.) Continue until pan is covered.

◆ Spread the spinach mixture in an 8-inch circle in the center of the pastry.

◆ Starting with the first folded sheet of pastry, bring the outside edge to the center and make a tight circle to enclose the filling. Repeat the folding process with the remaining pastry strips. Drizzle with the remaining butter.

◆ Bake at 375 degrees for 35 to 40 minutes or until golden brown.

◆ Cut into wedges. Serve warm or at room temperature.

 # Onion Strudel

Serves 6 to 8

4 medium red onions, sliced

3 tablespoons butter or margarine

2 tablespoons flour

pepper to taste

³/4 cup vegetable broth

¹/4 cup white wine

1¹/2 cup buttered plain croutons

1 cup shredded Swiss cheese

3 tablespoons grated Parmesan cheese

1 package phyllo pastry

1 cup melted butter

¹/4 cup yellow cornmeal

- ◆ Sauté the onions in 3 tablespoons butter in a skillet until tender.

- ◆ Stir in the flour and pepper. Mix in the broth and white wine.

- ◆ Cook over medium heat until thick and bubbly, stirring constantly.

- ◆ Let stand until cool. Stir in the croutons, Swiss cheese and Parmesan cheese.

- ◆ Place 6 sheets of the phyllo pastry on a work surface and cover with a damp towel to prevent drying out.

- ◆ Brush pastry 1 sheet at a time with melted butter and sprinkle lightly with cornmeal, stacking after completion of each sheet.

- ◆ Spread half the onion mixture to within 1 inch of the edge in the middle third of the pastry.

- ◆ Fold 1 end over the onion mixture. Roll as for a jelly roll. Place seam side down on a baking sheet. Brush with butter.

- ◆ Repeat the process with the remaining pastry, onion mixture and melted butter to make another strudel.

- ◆ Bake at 350 degrees for 35 to 45 minutes or until golden brown.

Wild Mushroom Tart

Serves 8 to 12

1 large red onion, thinly sliced

¼ cup olive oil

1 pint cremini mushrooms, sliced

½ cup Italian parsley leaves

1 tablespoon tomato paste

1 cup rich vegetable stock

salt and pepper to taste

3 eggs, beaten

½ cup grated Parmesan cheese

1 baked (9-inch) pie shell

◆ Sauté the onion in the olive oil in a skillet for 10 minutes or until tender. Stir in the mushrooms, parsley and tomato paste.

◆ Sauté for 5 minutes. Stir in the stock, salt and pepper.

◆ Cook until most of the broth has evaporated and the sauce has thickened, stirring frequently. Spoon into a bowl.

◆ Let stand until cool. Stir in the eggs and cheese. Spoon into the pie shell.

◆ Bake at 375 degrees for 20 minutes or until set.

◆ Let stand until cool. Cut into wedges.

Yellow Tomato and Onion Squares

Serves 12

10 slices white bread, crusts removed

4 cups thinly sliced onions

1/4 cup butter or margarine

8 ounces Gruyère cheese, grated

2 tablespoons flour

2 large yellow beefsteak tomatoes, cut into 1/4-inch slices

2 tablespoons thinly sliced fresh basil

1/2 cup milk or evaporated skim milk

2 extra-large eggs or equivalent amount of egg substitute

salt and freshly cracked pepper to taste

- ◆ Spray a 9x13-inch baking pan with nonstick cooking spray.

- ◆ Line the prepared pan with the bread to form a crust.

- ◆ Sauté the onions in the butter in a skillet until golden brown.

- ◆ Combine the cheese and flour in a bowl, tossing to coat.

- ◆ Sprinkle half the cheese mixture in the prepared pan. Layer the onions, sliced tomatoes, basil and remaining cheese mixture in the order listed over the prepared layers.

- ◆ Whisk the milk, eggs, salt and pepper in a bowl. Pour over the prepared layers.

- ◆ Chill for 15 minutes.

- ◆ Bake at 350 degrees for 35 to 45 minutes or until golden brown.

- ◆ Cut into squares.

 Zucchini Squares

Serves 12

8 medium zucchini, sliced

1¹/₂ cups chopped onion

8 cloves of garlic, chopped

3 tablespoons olive oil

1 cup grated Parmesan cheese

¹/₂ cup bread crumbs

2 eggs, beaten or equivalent
  amount of egg substitute

¹/₄ cup chopped fresh basil

1 teaspoon freshly ground or
  cracked pepper

grated Parmesan cheese to taste

◆ Steam the zucchini in a steamer for 10 minutes.
  Drain and mash to remove excess moisture.

◆ Sauté the onion and garlic in the olive oil in a skillet
  until light brown. Add the zucchini.

◆ Cook until zucchini is heated through, stirring
  constantly. Remove from heat.

◆ Whisk 1 cup Parmesan cheese, bread crumbs,
  eggs, basil and pepper in a bowl. Stir in the
  zucchini mixture.

◆ Spoon into a greased 9x13-inch baking dish.
  Sprinkle with Parmesan cheese to taste.

◆ Bake at 375 degrees for 30 minutes.

◆ Let stand until cool. Cut into bite-size squares.

Soups • Salads

 # Lauren's Gazpacho

Serves 6

1 (24-ounce) can vegetable juice cocktail

1 cup water

3 beef or vegetable bouillon cubes

¼ cup red wine vinegar

3 tablespoons olive oil

1 teaspoon Tabasco sauce

1 bunch scallions, trimmed, coarsely chopped

1 green pepper, coarsely chopped

1 large cucumber, seeded, coarsely chopped

salt and freshly ground pepper to taste

chopped tomatoes

chopped cucumbers

chopped scallions

seasoned croutons

◆ Combine the vegetable juice cocktail, water and bouillon cubes in a saucepan.

◆ Heat until the bouillon dissolves, stirring occasionally. Stir in the wine vinegar, olive oil and Tabasco sauce.

◆ Combine 1 bunch scallions, green pepper and 1 cucumber in a food processor container. Add some of the bouillon mixture.

◆ Process until of the consistency of a thick broth. Pour into a bowl. Stir in the remaining bouillon mixture.

◆ Chill, covered, until serving time. Season with salt and pepper.

◆ Ladle into soup bowls. Top each serving with chopped tomatoes, chopped cucumbers, chopped scallions and croutons.

 Curried Pea Soup

Serves 6 to 8

6 cups strong chicken broth

3 cups cooked fresh or frozen
   green peas

2¹/₂ tablespoons curry powder

freshly cracked pepper

³/₄ cup evaporated skim milk

2 eggs or equivalent amount of
   egg substitute

1 green apple, thinly sliced

- ◆ Combine the broth, green peas, curry powder and pepper in a food processor container.

- ◆ Process until smooth. Pour into a heavy 2-quart saucepan.

- ◆ Cook just until heated through, stirring frequently.

- ◆ Mix the skim milk and eggs in a bowl. Add to the pea mixture gradually, stirring constantly.

- ◆ Cook just until thickened, stirring constantly. Remove from heat.

- ◆ Chill, covered, until serving time. Whisk just before serving.

- ◆ Ladle into soup bowls. Top each serving with apple slices.

Potato Leek Soup

Serves 6 to 8

6 leek bulbs, thinly sliced

3 tablespoons olive oil

5 medium potatoes, peeled, cut into ¹/₂-inch pieces

6 cups strong chicken stock

1¹/₂ cups evaporated skim milk

³/₄ cup light sour cream

salt and freshly cracked pepper to taste

¹/₄ cup chopped fresh chives

- ◆ Sauté the leeks in the olive oil in a saucepan until tender. Add the potatoes.

- ◆ Sauté for 2 to 3 minutes.

- ◆ Bring the stock to a boil in a saucepan. Stir in the leek mixture.

- ◆ Cook over medium heat for 30 minutes or until the potatoes and leeks are tender, stirring occasionally.

- ◆ Let stand until cool.

- ◆ Process the potato mixture in batches in a food processor until smooth. Pour into a bowl. Whisk in the skim milk and sour cream. Season with salt and pepper.

- ◆ Ladle into soup bowls. Sprinkle with chives.

Note:
This soup may be served hot or cold.

 # Tomato Basil Soup

Serves 4

4¹/₂ cups chopped seeded peeled tomatoes

1 cup chopped onion

1 cup vegetable broth

1 tablespoon fresh lemon juice

1 teaspoon sugar (optional)

¹/₂ teaspoon freshly cracked pepper

¹/₂ cup chopped fresh basil leaves (10 to 20 leaves)

◆ Sauté the tomatoes and onion in a Dutch oven sprayed with nonstick vegetable or olive oil cooking spray until tender.

◆ Add the broth, lemon juice, sugar and pepper and mix well.

◆ Simmer, covered, for 30 minutes, stirring occasionally.

◆ Let stand until cool.

◆ Process the tomato mixture in batches in a food processor or blender until of a coarse consistency; do not purée. Pour into a bowl. Stir in the basil.

◆ Chill slightly. Ladle into soup bowls.

Note:
Spoon over the pasta of your choice and sprinkle with grated Parmesan cheese for a great vegetarian entrée.

 # Cuban Banana Soup

Serves 4

1 (12-ounce) package dried banana chips

8 cups strong chicken broth

- ◆ Process the banana chips in a food processor or blender until almost a powder.

- ◆ Bring the chicken broth to a boil in a saucepan; reduce heat to medium. Stir in the banana powder.

- ◆ Cook for 20 minutes, stirring frequently. The soup will thicken and has a glossy appearance.

- ◆ Ladle into soup bowls.

 Black Bean Soup   Serves 6 to 8

1 pound dried black beans

3 quarts water

3 cups chopped onions

2 cups chopped celery

1 cup chopped yellow or orange
   bell pepper

6 cloves of garlic, finely chopped

3 scallions, finely chopped

2 tablespoons olive oil

8 cups chicken or vegetable
   broth

1 cup packed Italian parsley
   leaves

1/2 cup packed chopped fresh
   cilantro

4 large bay leaves, crumbled

1 teaspoon oregano

1 teaspoon cumin

salt and pepper to taste

chopped scallions

- Sort and rinse the black beans. Combine the beans and water in a large bowl.

- Let stand for 8 to 10 hours. Drain, reserving 2 cups of the liquid.

- Sauté the onions, celery, bell pepper, garlic and 3 scallions in the olive oil in a stockpot until tender. Add the beans and mix well.

- Stir in the broth, parsley, cilantro, bay leaves, oregano, cumin and reserved liquid.

- Bring to a boil; reduce heat.

- Simmer, covered, for 3 to 3 1/2 hours or until the beans are tender, stirring occasionally. Season with salt and pepper.

- Ladle into soup bowls. Sprinkle with chopped scallions.

Beer and Broccoli Cheese Soup

Serves 6 to 8

¹/₂ cup chopped celery

¹/₂ cup chopped onion

¹/₂ cup chopped carrots

¹/₂ cup butter or margarine

¹/₃ cup flour

florets of 1 bunch broccoli

5 cups rich chicken broth

1¹/₂ cups beer

2 cups shredded Cheddar cheese

1 teaspoon all purpose Greek
seasoning/salt-free

¹/₂ teaspoon dry mustard

freshly cracked pepper to taste

- Sauté the celery, onion and carrots in the butter in a saucepan until tender. Stir in the flour.

- Combine the broccoli and half the broth in a saucepan. Bring to a boil; reduce heat.

- Simmer, covered, for 7 minutes. Drain, reserving the liquid; coarsely chop the broccoli.

- Combine the celery mixture, reserved liquid, remaining broth and beer in a stockpot and mix well. Stir in the broccoli.

- Add the cheese, Greek seasoning, dry mustard and pepper and mix gently.

- Heat just until the cheese melts, stirring frequently; do not boil.

- Ladle into soup bowls.

 # Chicken Soup

Serves 6

2 (3-pound) chickens, cut up
1¹/₂ teaspoons salt
freshly ground pepper to taste
2 large onions, cut into quarters
3 large carrots, peeled, sliced
1 large parsnip, peeled
4 large ribs celery with leaves
¹/₂ bunch fresh parsley
salt to taste

- Combine the chicken, 1¹/₂ teaspoons salt and pepper with enough water to cover in a stockpot.

- Bring to a boil; skim top. Add the onions, carrots, parsnip and celery.

- Simmer, covered, for 2¹/₂ hours or until the chicken is tender, stirring occasionally.

- Tie the parsley stems together with kitchen twine to make for easy removal. Add to the stockpot.

- Cook for 15 minutes longer, stirring occasionally. Taste and add salt to taste and pepper if desired.

- Strain the broth, reserving the carrots and chicken and discarding the remaining vegetables and parsley. Return the broth and carrots to the stockpot.

- Chop the chicken, discarding the skin and bones. Add to the stockpot and mix well.

- Chill, covered, in the refrigerator. Skim the fat.

- Cook just until heated through, stirring occasionally.

- Ladle into soup bowls.

Chicken Soup with Fresh Spinach Pasta   Serves 8

16 cups water

3 pounds chicken wings

1 pound chicken thighs

1 bunch celery, chopped

5 carrots, peeled, cut into quarters

3 yellow onions, cut into 8 pieces

2 tomatoes, cut into halves

1/2 bunch Italian parsley

3 cloves of garlic

8 whole black peppercorns

8 ounces fresh spinach pasta

1/2 cup freshly grated Parmesan cheese

- ◆ Combine the water, chicken wings, chicken thighs, celery, carrots, onions, tomatoes, parsley, garlic and peppercorns in a stockpot. Bring to boil; reduce heat.
- ◆ Simmer for 2 hours, stirring occasionally.
- ◆ Strain the broth into a saucepan, discarding the chicken, vegetables and seasonings.
- ◆ Chill, covered, in the refrigerator; skim.
- ◆ Bring to a simmer. Add the pasta.
- ◆ Cook until the pasta is tender, stirring occasionally.
- ◆ Ladle into soup bowls. Sprinkle with the cheese.

Note:
The broth may be prepared 1 day in advance and stored, covered, in the refrigerator. Add the noodles just before serving.

New England Clam Chowder

Serves 4

4 ribs celery, sliced

1 large onion, chopped

2 cloves of garlic, minced

3 tablespoons olive oil

3 tablespoons flour

1 small bay leaf

1 small bunch parsley, chopped

$1/2$ teaspoon salt

$1/2$ teaspoon pepper

2 cups cream or evaporated skim milk

2 medium potatoes, peeled, chopped

2 cans minced clams

1 can whole clams

- ◆ Sauté the celery, onion and garlic in the olive oil in a saucepan until tender.

- ◆ Add the flour, bay leaf, parsley, salt and pepper, stirring until mixed.

- ◆ Stir in the cream, potatoes and undrained clams.

- ◆ Simmer for 30 to 40 minutes or until the potatoes are tender. Discard the bay leaf.

- ◆ Ladle into soup bowls.

 # Crab Bisque

Serves 6

1½ ribs celery, chopped

1 medium onion, chopped

1 large carrot, chopped

¼ cup vegetable oil

1 pound fresh or frozen crab meat

1½ teaspoons paprika

¾ teaspoon salt

¾ teaspoon pepper

1 (10-ounce) can cream of mushroom soup

1 (10-ounce) can cream of celery soup

2 soup cans half-and-half or evaporated skim milk

½ cup dry white wine

1 tablespoon butter or margarine (optional)

½ cup chopped fresh parsley

◆ Sauté the celery, onion and carrot in the oil in a saucepan until tender. Stir in the crab meat, paprika, salt and pepper.

◆ Simmer for 20 minutes, stirring occasionally.

◆ Add the soups and mix well. Pour into a food processor or blender container.

◆ Process until smooth. Return to the saucepan. Stir in the half-and-half and white wine.

◆ Cook just until heated through, stirring frequently.

◆ Ladle into soup bowls. Top with each serving with ½ teaspoon butter and sprinkle with parsley.

Onion Soup Gratin

Serves 6

6 (1-inch) slices French bread

4 large onions, thinly sliced

2 cloves of garlic, crushed

1/4 cup vegetable oil

2 tablespoons flour

6 cups strong homemade or
 canned chicken stock

1/2 cup white wine

1 teaspoon thyme

salt and pepper to taste

2 cups grated Gruyère or
 Parmesan cheese

◆ Arrange the bread slices on a baking sheet.

◆ Bake in a moderate oven just until dry; do
 not brown.

◆ Sauté the onions and garlic in the oil in a saucepan
 until the onions are light brown. Sprinkle with
 the flour.

◆ Cook over low heat until mixed, stirring constantly;
 do not brown. Stir in the stock and white wine.

◆ Bring to a boil, stirring constantly. Add the thyme,
 salt and pepper and mix well.

◆ Simmer for 20 minutes, stirring occasionally.

◆ Place the bread slices in ovenproof soup bowls or
 ramekins. Pour the soup over the bread; sprinkle
 with the cheese.

◆ Place the soup bowls on a baking sheet.

◆ Broil until the cheese melts.

Variation:
May substitute a mixture of 3 cups chicken stock and 3
cups beef stock for the chicken stock.

Oyster Artichoke Soup

Serves 4

2 pints oysters

2 chicken bouillon cubes

1/4 cup butter

1/4 cup flour

1/2 cup sliced green onions

2 teaspoons chopped fresh parsley

1/2 teaspoon thyme

1/2 teaspoon salt

1/2 teaspoon cayenne

1 cup whipping cream

1 (14-ounce) can artichoke hearts, drained, cut into quarters

- ◆ Drain the oysters, reserving the liquid. Combine the reserved liquid with enough water to measure 3 cups.

- ◆ Combine the oyster liquid and bouillon cubes in a saucepan. Bring to a boil; reduce heat.

- ◆ Simmer for 8 to 10 minutes, stirring occasionally.

- ◆ Heat the butter in a saucepan until melted. Whisk in the flour.

- ◆ Cook for 2 to 3 minutes, stirring constantly.

- ◆ Add the green onions, parsley, thyme, salt and cayenne and mix well. Whisk in the oyster liquid mixture and whipping cream gradually.

- ◆ Cook until thickened, stirring constantly; do not boil. Reduce heat.

- ◆ Stir in the oysters and artichokes.

- ◆ Simmer until the edges of the oysters curl. Remove from heat.

- ◆ Ladle into soup bowls.

Pasta e Fagioli

Serves 6

2 cups dried cranberry beans

2 extra-large yellow onions, chopped

4 medium carrots, chopped

4 ribs celery, chopped

3 large cloves of garlic, smashed, chopped

2 tablespoons chopped fresh rosemary

1 tablespoon chopped fresh basil

2 teaspoons dried sage

freshly ground pepper to taste

10 cups low-sodium chicken stock

8 ounces fettuccini, cooked, drained, cut into 1-inch pieces

- ◆ Sort and rinse the beans. Combine the beans with enough water to cover in a bowl.

- ◆ Let stand for 8 to 10 hours; drain.

- ◆ Combine the onions, carrots, celery, garlic, rosemary, basil, sage and pepper in a large heavy stockpot and cover.

- ◆ Sweat for 10 minutes, stirring occasionally. Stir in the beans.

- ◆ Add the stock to cover the bean mixture by approximately 1 inch. Add water if the mixture is not covered. Bring to a boil; reduce to medium simmer.

- ◆ Cook for 2 to 3 hours or until the beans are tender, adding water and stirring occasionally as needed. The bean mixture should be covered with liquid during the entire cooking process.

- ◆ Cool slightly.

- ◆ Process 3/4 of the soup in a food processor until smooth. Return to the stockpot and mix well.

- ◆ Cook just until heated through, stirring frequently. Stir in the fettuccini just before serving.

- ◆ Ladle into soup bowls.

 # Yellow Pea Soup

Serves 4 to 6

8 ounces yellow split peas

6 cups water

1 teaspoon salt

1 teaspoon oregano

3 cloves of garlic, chopped

1/4 teaspoon red pepper flakes

1/3 cup olive oil

1 cup dry white wine (optional)

2 to 3 cups very rich chicken broth or water

Juice of 1 lemon

3 scallions, chopped

1/4 cup chopped fresh dillweed

- ◆ Sort and rinse the peas. Combine the peas, water and salt in a stockpot.

- ◆ Bring to a boil; skim peas and shells that float to the top. Stir in the oregano.

- ◆ Simmer for 30 to 45 minutes or until the peas are tender, stirring frequently. The peas are cooked through when they turn into a smooth paste when stirred. Add additional water as needed.

- ◆ Cool for 15 minutes.

- ◆ Sauté the garlic and red pepper flakes in 2 table-spoons of the olive oil in a saucepan. Stir in the white wine. Add the peas and mix well.

- ◆ Add the broth, stirring until of a creamy consistency.

- ◆ Cook just until heated through, stirring frequently. Stir in the desired amount of the remaining olive oil, lemon juice and scallions just before serving.

- ◆ Ladle into soup bowls. Sprinkle with the dillweed.

 Destin Seafood Gumbo

Serves 12

¹/₄ cup olive oil

6 tablespoons flour

2 large onions, chopped

2 cups chopped celery

1 gallon chicken stock

4 cups sliced fresh okra

1 pound fresh or frozen crab meat

2 pints select oysters

3 fresh tomatoes, peeled, chopped

1 can tomato sauce

4 green onions, chopped

6 cloves of garlic, minced

3 tablespoons thyme

3 tablespoons basil

2 tablespoons Worcestershire sauce

2 tablespoons parsley

2 tablespoons all purpose Greek seasoning/salt-free

1 tablespoon paprika

6 peppercorns

4 bay leaves

4 allspice balls (optional)

pepper to taste

3 cups cooked rice

- Heat the olive oil in a heavy skillet. Add the flour gradually, stirring constantly.

- Cook over low heat until the mixture is a deep brown, stirring constantly. Stir in the onions and celery.

- Cook for 30 minutes, stirring frequently.

- Combine the onion mixture, stock, okra, crab meat, oysters, tomatoes, tomato sauce, green onions, garlic, thyme, basil, Worcestershire sauce, parsley, Greek seasoning, paprika, peppercorns, bay leaves and allspice balls in a stockpot and mix well.

- Simmer for 3 hours or longer, stirring occasionally. Stir in the rice.

- Cook until thickened and of the desired consistency, stirring frequently. Discard the bay leaves.

- Ladle into soup bowls.

Picnic Shrimp Stew

Serves 6

1½ quarts chicken stock

1 pound andouille sausage, cut diagonally into 1-inch pieces

1 large onion, sliced

½ fennel bulb, cut into quarters

1 bay leaf

1 tablespoon thyme

3 ears fresh corn, cut into quarters

1 red bell pepper, roasted, peeled, cut into 1-inch pieces

1 yellow bell pepper, roasted, peeled, cut into 1-inch pieces

salt and freshly ground pepper to taste

24 large fresh peeled Gulf shrimp with tails

⅓ pound thin fresh green beans

freshly chopped fennel top

◆ Bring the stock to a boil in a stockpot. Add the sausage.

◆ Boil gently for 20 minutes. Remove the sausage with a slotted spoon to a bowl. Cover to keep warm.

◆ Add the onion, fennel bulb, bay leaf and thyme to the stock and mix well.

◆ Simmer, loosely covered, for 20 minutes or until the onion and fennel are tender, stirring occasionally. Add the corn and bell peppers.

◆ Cook for 15 minutes or until the corn is tender, stirring occasionally. Season with salt and pepper.

◆ Bring to a boil. Add the shrimp and green beans.

◆ Cook, covered, for 5 minutes or until the shrimp turn pink; do not overcook the shrimp. Remove from heat. Discard the bay leaf.

◆ Place 4 shrimp, 2 pieces of corn, sausage and some of the fennel, bell peppers, onions and green beans in each of 6 soup bowls. Ladle the broth over the mixture. Sprinkle with chopped fennel top.

Neighborhood Vegetable Soup

Serves 6 to 8

1 large onion, chopped

1 cup sliced carrot

1 cup chopped celery

½ cup chopped parsnips

1 leek bulk, chopped

2 cloves of garlic, chopped

¼ cup vegetable oil

1 cup sliced fresh green beans

1 cup chopped potato

1 cup fresh corn kernels

5 cups water or vegetable, chicken or beef broth

1 (6- to 8-ounce) envelope vegetable or minestrone soup mix

9 black peppercorns

1 teaspoon salt (optional)

1 bay leaf

2 cups cooked pasta (not spaghetti)

- ◆ Sauté the onion, carrot, celery, parsnips, leek and garlic in the oil in a saucepan; reduce heat.

- ◆ Cook over low heat for 20 minutes, stirring frequently. Stir in the green beans, potato and corn. Add the water and soup mix and mix well. Stir in the peppercorns, salt and bay leaf. Bring to a boil; reduce heat.

- ◆ Simmer, covered, for 1 hour, stirring occasionally. May add additional water if needed. Discard the bay leaf.

- ◆ Stir in the pasta. Adjust seasonings.

- ◆ Ladle into soup bowls.

# Southwest Black Bean Salad

Serves 6

2 cups dried black beans

1¹/₂ cups chopped purple onion

1 (16-ounce) can chick-peas, drained

1 large tomato, seeded, chopped

1 medium orange or yellow bell pepper, chopped

1 cup fresh corn kernels

¹/₄ cup olive oil

¹/₄ cup fresh lime juice

¹/₄ cup chopped fresh cilantro

¹/₄ cup chopped fresh parsley

6 cloves of garlic, finely chopped

2 tablespoons chili powder

1 teaspoon red pepper flakes, crushed

¹/₂ teaspoon cumin

salt and pepper to taste

- ◆ Sort and rinse the beans. Combine the beans with enough cold water to cover in a bowl.

- ◆ Let stand for 3 hours or longer. Drain, discarding any discolored beans; rinse.

- ◆ Combine the beans with enough water to cover in a stockpot.

- ◆ Cook until tender, stirring occasionally; drain.

- ◆ Let stand until cool.

- ◆ Combine the beans, onion, chick-peas, tomato, bell pepper, corn, olive oil, lime juice, cilantro, parsley, garlic, chili powder, red pepper flakes, cumin, salt and pepper in a bowl and mix gently.

Hearts of Palm Salad with Balsamic and Basil Vinaigrette

Serves 6 to 8

For the Balsamic and Basil Vinaigrette

$1/2$ cup water

$1/2$ cup olive oil

$1/2$ cup balsamic vinegar

$1/2$ cup chopped fresh parsley

$1/4$ cup orange juice

6 tablespoons chopped shallot

2 teaspoons chopped garlic

2 teaspoons Dijon mustard

For the Salad

1 bunch purple leaf lettuce

1 (14-ounce) can hearts of palm

1 small red onion, thinly sliced

1 (16-ounce) can garbanzo
   beans, drained

1 pint fresh sprouts

- To prepare the vinaigrette, combine the water, olive oil, balsamic vinegar, parsley, orange juice, shallot, garlic, and Dijon mustard in a food processor or blender container.

- Process until of the desired consistency. May add additional water for a thinner consistency.

- To prepare the salad, rinse the lettuce and pat dry.

- Place 2 lettuce leafs and 1 stalk of palm on each salad plate. Arrange the onion around the palm.

- Sprinkle with the beans and top with the sprouts.

- Drizzle with the desired amount of the vinaigrette. Serve immediately.

 Crunchy Slaw

Serves 8

For the Creamy Dressing

³/₄ cup light sour cream

¹/₂ cup low-fat mayonnaise

2 tablespoons Dijon mustard

2 tablespoons rice wine vinegar
    or cider vinegar

freshly ground pepper to taste

For the Slaw

5 cups shredded red cabbage

5 cups shredded green cabbage

2 cups shredded carrots

1 cup chopped scallions

1 green apple, chopped

◆ To prepare the dressing, combine the sour cream, mayonnaise, Dijon mustard, rice wine vinegar and pepper in a bowl and mix well.

◆ To prepare the slaw, toss the red and green cabbage in a bowl.

◆ Add the carrots and scallions and mix well. Mix in the apple.

◆ Pour the dressing over the slaw, tossing to coat.

◆ Chill, covered, until serving time.

 # Spinach Salad

Serves 8

For the Dressing

1 cup canola oil

³/₄ cup red wine vinegar

¹/₂ cup sugar

1 tablespoon soy sauce

For the Salad

2 pounds fresh spinach

2 cups sliced fresh mushrooms

2 cups sliced fresh strawberries

4 hard-cooked eggs, sliced (optional)

1 red onion, sliced

1 cup chopped walnuts (optional)

4 slices apple-smoked bacon, crumbled (optional)

◆ For the dressing, combine the canola oil, wine vinegar, sugar and soy sauce in a jar with a tightfitting lid and shake to mix.

◆ Store in the refrigerator.

◆ For the salad, rinse the spinach and pat dry.

◆ Combine the spinach, mushrooms, strawberries and eggs in a salad bowl and mix gently.

◆ Add the dressing, tossing to coat.

◆ Top with the onion, walnuts and bacon.

Wild Rice and Artichoke Salad

Serves 6

1 (6-ounce) package long grain
  and wild rice
2 (6-ounce) jars marinated
  artichoke quarters
$^1/_4$ cup low-fat mayonnaise
$^1/_4$ cup light sour cream
1 teaspoon cracked pepper
$^1/_2$ teaspoon curry powder
6 green onions, sliced diagonally
  into $^1/_2$-inch pieces
$^1/_4$ red bell pepper, julienned
$^1/_4$ yellow bell pepper, julienned
$^1/_4$ cup sliced black olives

◆ Cook the rice using package directions.

◆ Let stand until cool.

◆ Drain the artichokes, reserving the liquid.

◆ Combine the reserved liquid, mayonnaise, sour
  cream, pepper and curry powder in a bowl and
  mix well.

◆ Combine the artichokes, green onions, red pepper,
  yellow pepper and olives in a bowl and mix gently.
  Add the mayonnaise mixture and toss gently.

◆ Chill, covered, in the refrigerator until serving time.

Note:
May be prepared in advance and stored, covered, in
the refrigerator.

Chopped Vegetable Salad

Serves 6 to 8

2 large ripe tomatoes, seeded, chopped

2 cucumbers, peeled, seeded, chopped

1 yellow bell pepper, chopped

1 medium red onion, chopped

6 cloves of garlic, chopped

1½ cups drained chick-peas

1 cup crumbled feta cheese

1 cup black Greek olives, chopped

1 cup finely chopped fresh parsley

⅓ cup chopped fresh basil

1 teaspoon oregano

⅓ cup (about) olive oil

Juice of 1 to 2 lemons

salt and freshly ground pepper to taste

◆ Place the tomatoes, cucumbers, yellow pepper, onion and garlic in colander to drain.

◆ Combine the drained vegetables, chick-peas, feta cheese and olives in a bowl and toss to mix. Add the parsley, basil and oregano and mix well.

◆ Add the olive oil and lemon juice, tossing to coat. Season with salt and pepper.

Note:

Serve as an antipasto salad or add 4 cups chopped romaine lettuce and serve as a main dish salad. May decrease the amount of olive oil if desired.

 # Grilled Salad with Infused Oil

Serves 4

For the Dressing

³/₄ cup extra-virgin olive oil

1 cup chopped fresh parsley

¹/₄ cup chopped fresh chives

¹/₂ cup raspberry vinegar

For the Salad

2 portobello mushrooms, grilled, julienned

2 eggplant slices, grilled, julienned

12 asparagus spears, grilled

8 ounces asiago cheese, cubed

1 cup coarsely chopped walnuts

- ◆ To prepare the dressing, pour the olive oil into a blender container.

- ◆ Add the parsley and chives.

- ◆ Process on High until smooth. Add the raspberry vinegar.

- ◆ Process until blended.

- ◆ To prepare the salad, arrange ¹/₄ of the mushrooms, eggplant, asparagus, cheese and walnuts on each of 4 salad plates.

- ◆ Drizzle with the desired amount of the dressing. Serve the remaining dressing on the side.

 Curried Chicken Salad   Serves 4

For the Dressing

3 cups mayonnaise, sour cream
   or plain yogurt

1 to 2 tablespoons sugar

2 teaspoons curry powder

For the Salad

2 (10-ounce) packages frozen
   peas, thawed

3 cups chopped cooked chicken

2 cups seeded sliced cucumbers

1¹/₂ cups seedless green grape
   halves

1 cup salted peanuts

3 cups lightly seasoned croutons

6 cups shredded lettuce

◆ To prepare the dressing, combine the mayonnaise,
   sugar and curry powder in a bowl and mix well. Add
   water or milk for a thinner consistency.

◆ To prepare the salad, combine the peas, chicken,
   cucumbers, grapes and peanuts in a bowl and
   mix well.

◆ Add the dressing and croutons, tossing to mix.

◆ Spoon the chicken salad onto 4 lettuce-lined
   salad plates.

Note:
May substitute a mixture of 1¹/₂ cups mayonnaise and
1¹/₂ cups sour cream for 3 cups mayonnaise, sour
cream or yogurt.

# Seafood Garden Salad

Serves 4

For the Dressing

1/2 cup extra-virgin olive oil

1/4 cup balsamic vinegar

1 tablespoon sugar

1 teaspoon minced garlic

salt and freshly ground pepper
   to taste

For the Salad

6 cups mixed salad greens

2 cups finely shredded cabbage

1 (14-ounce) can hearts of palm,
   drained, sliced

1 cup trimmed green beans, cut
   into halves, blanched

1 red bell pepper, roasted,
   peeled, julienned

1 yellow bell pepper, roasted,
   peeled, julienned

1/2 cup chopped green onions

1 pound fresh shrimp, cooked,
   peeled, deveined, butterflied

toasted sesame seeds

◆ For the dressing, whisk the olive oil, balsamic vinegar, sugar, garlic, salt and pepper in a bowl until mixed.

◆ For the salad, mix the salad greens, cabbage, hearts of palm, green beans, red pepper, yellow pepper and green onions in a bowl.

◆ Add the dressing and toss to coat.

◆ Arrange the salad green mixture evenly on 4 salad plates. Top with the shrimp. Sprinkle with sesame seeds.

Variation:
Substitute 1 pound julienned grilled chicken breast for the shrimp.

 Salad Niçoise

Serves 6

For the Dressing

1 cup olive oil

¹/₂ cup red wine vinegar

¹/₄ cup drained capers

¹/₄ cup chopped green onions

2 teaspoons dried basil

2 teaspoons dried marjoram

2 teaspoons dried oregano

2 teaspoons dried thyme

¹/₂ teaspoon dry mustard

¹/₂ teaspoon freshly cracked
pepper

salt to taste

For the Salad

6 unpeeled red potatoes

3 cups thin fresh green beans

1 to 2 bunches romaine, chilled

4 cups drained water-pack tuna,
chilled, flaked

1 (2-ounce) can anchovy fillets,
chilled, drained

5 hard-cooked eggs, chilled, cut
into quarters

5 tomatoes, chilled, cut into
wedges

1¹/₂ cups sliced black olives

- To prepare the dressing, combine the olive oil, wine vinegar, capers, green onions, basil, marjoram, oregano, thyme, dry mustard, pepper and salt in a jar with a tightfiting lid and shake to mix.

- To prepare the salad, place the red potatoes in a saucepan. Add boiling water to measure 1 inch.

- Cook for 15 minutes or until tender. Drain and slice.

- Place the green beans in a saucepan. Add boiling water to measure 2 inches.

- Cook for 3 minutes; drain.

- Mix the hot potatoes and hot green beans in a bowl. Pour ¹/₂ cup of the dressing over the mixture, tossing to coat.

- Marinate in the refrigerator for 30 minutes or longer.

- To assemble, line a large salad platter with some of the romaine lettuce. Arrange the marinated vegetables on the lettuce.

- Tear the remaining romaine lettuce into bite-size pieces and place on the platter.

- Mound the tuna in the center of the greens. Arrange the anchovies around the tuna. Place the egg and tomato wedges around the outer edge of the platter. Top with the olives.

- Serve with the remaining dressing.

Spicy Blender Dressing

Makes 3 cups

1¹⁄₃ cups extra-virgin olive oil

1 cup packed fresh parsley

³⁄₄ cup raspberry vinegar

¹⁄₄ cup grated Parmesan cheese
   (optional)

3 tablespoons mixed green herbs
   (basil, thyme, marjoram,
   oregano, parsley)

2 large green onions, chopped

2 tablespoons minced garlic

1 tablespoon freshly cracked
   pepper

1 tablespoons capers

1 tablespoon fresh lemon juice

1 tablespoon sugar

1 teaspoon Dijon mustard

◆ Combine the olive oil, parsley, raspberry vinegar,
  cheese, herbs, green onions, garlic, pepper, capers,
  lemon juice, sugar and Dijon mustard in a blender
  or food processor container.

◆ Process until blended.

◆ Add cold water 1 tablespoon at a time for a thinner
  consistency.

Note:
Use as marinade for chicken, lamb or vegetables as
well as a dressing for salads.

Caesar Salad Dressing

Makes 1 cup

¹⁄₂ cup extra-virgin olive oil

3 tablespoons grated Parmesan
   cheese

1 (2-ounce) can anchovy fillets

Juice of 3 lemons

3 cloves of garlic

1 tablespoon Dijon mustard

¹⁄₂ teaspoon freshly cracked
   pepper

¹⁄₂ teaspoon Worcestershire
   sauce

◆ Combine the olive oil, cheese, anchovies,
  lemon juice, garlic, Dijon mustard, pepper and
  Worcestershire sauce in a blender or food
  processor container.

◆ Process until blended. Taste and adjust seasonings.

Main Dishes

 Roasted Beef Brisket

Serves 6 to 8

1 tablespoon all-purpose Greek seasoning/salt-free

1 tablespoon Beau Monde seasoning

salt and freshly cracked pepper to taste

1 (5- to 6-pound) beef brisket, trimmed

2 envelopes onion soup mix

2 large onions, sliced

1 head of garlic, peeled, crushed

3 cups water or red wine

3 carrots, peeled, sliced

3 ribs celery, sliced

1 cup chopped fresh parsley

1/3 cup catsup

sliced carrots

sliced celery

sliced potatoes

◆ Mix the Greek seasoning, Beau Monde seasoning, salt and pepper in a bowl. Rub over the surface of the brisket.

◆ Combine the soup mix with the specified amount of water stated on the package in a roasing pan. Mix in the onions and garlic. Place the brisket in the pan.

◆ Add 3 cups water, 3 carrots, 3 ribs celery, parsley and catsup and mix well.

◆ Roast, covered, at 325 degrees for 2 1/2 hours or until almost cooked through. Remove the brisket to a platter. Cool slightly.

◆ Skim the broth and strain, discarding the onions, carrots and celery. Slice the brisket.

◆ Return the brisket, broth, sliced carrots, sliced celery and sliced potatoes to the roasting pan.

◆ Roast, covered, for 40 minutes longer or until the brisket and vegetables are tender.

 Barbequed Flank Steak   Serves 4

1/2 **cup vegetable oil or fat-free balsamic salad dressing**

1/4 **cup chopped fresh parsley**

1/4 **cup soy sauce**

3 **scallions, chopped**

3 **tablespoons honey**

2 **tablespoons balsamic vinegar**

1 **tablespoon all purpose Greek seasoning/salt-free**

4 **cloves of garlic, chopped**

1 1/2 **teaspoons ginger**

1 **(1 1/2-pound) flank steak**

- ◆ Combine the oil, parsley, soy sauce, scallions, honey, balsamic vinegar, Greek seasoning, garlic and ginger in a bowl and mix well.

- ◆ Pour the oil mixture over the steak in a shallow dish, turning to coat.

- ◆ Marinate, covered, in the refrigerator for 2 to 10 hours, turning occasionally. (The longer the marinating time the more tender the steak.)

- ◆ Grill on a gas grill on High for 7 to 9 minutes per side for rare, turning once. Add 1 to 2 minutes per side for medium.

- ◆ Let rest for 2 to 3 minutes.

- ◆ Slice against the grain at a slight angle to the desired thickness.

 Pan-Seared Peppercorn Steak

Serves 2 to 4

For the Steaks

3 tablespoons freshly cracked pepper

2 New York strip steaks, 1¼ inches thick

For the Ragout

1 pound mushrooms, sliced

1 medium onion, sliced

¼ cup olive oil

1 (10-ounce) can low-sodium beef broth

2 cups red wine

1 large tomato, peeled, seeded, chopped

⅛ teaspoon nutmeg

2 to 4 tablespoons butter or margarine

◆ For the steaks, press the pepper over both sides of the steaks.

◆ Spray a heavy skillet generously with nonstick cooking spray. Heat the skillet on high until hot. Add the steaks.

◆ Sear the steaks on both sides.

◆ Cook the steaks on medium-high for 4 minutes and turn. Cook for 4 minutes or until of the desired degree of doneness; turn. Cook for 4 minutes longer. Turn the steaks on their sides and sear for 2 to 4 minutes longer if fat is visible.

◆ Remove to a heated serving platter. Cover to keep warm.

◆ For the ragout, sauté the mushrooms and onion in the olive oil in a skillet for 10 minutes. Add the broth, red wine, tomato and nutmeg and mix well. Bring to a gentle boil; reduce to a medium simmer.

◆ Simmer until the mixture measures 1 cup, stirring frequently.

◆ Add the butter 1 tablespoon at a time, mixing well after each addition. Spoon over the steak.

Top Sirloin with Green Peppercorn and Mustard Sauce

Serves 2 to 4

1¹/₂ tablespoons drained green peppercorns in brine

1¹/₂ tablespoons Dijon mustard

1 tablespoon unsalted butter, softened

2 teaspoons flour

1 (15-to 16-ounce) top sirloin steak, 1¹/₄ inches thick

salt and pepper to taste

1¹/₂ tablespoons vegetable oil

¹/₂ cup canned beef broth

¹/₄ cup whipping cream

◆ Mash the peppercorns in a bowl with the bottom of a heavy glass. Stir in the Dijon mustard, butter and flour. May be prepared 1 day in advance and stored, covered, in the refrigerator.

◆ Season the steak on both sides with salt and pepper.

◆ Heat the oil in a skillet over high heat. Add the steak.

◆ Cook for 5 minutes per side for rare or until of the desired degree of doneness, turning once.

◆ Remove the steak to a heated platter and tent with foil to keep warm.

◆ Discard the pan drippings. Stir the broth and whipping cream into the same skillet. Bring to a boil.

◆ Boil for 3 minutes or until slightly thickened, stirring constantly to loosen any browned bits. Stir in the peppercorn mixture.

◆ Boil for 1 minute or until the mixture coats a spoon, whisking constantly. Season with salt and pepper. Remove from heat.

◆ Cut the steak crosswise into thin slices.

◆ Arrange the slices on individual dinner plates. Spoon the sauce over the steak.

Grilled T-bone Steak with Garlic and Chili Butter

Serves 4

For the Garlic and Chili Butter

2 fresh Anaheim chiles

6 unpeeled cloves of garlic

2 tablespoons olive oil

$^1/_4$ cup unsalted butter, softened

1 teaspoon chili powder

1 teaspoon Tabasco sauce

For the Steaks

4 T-bone steaks, $1^1/_4$ inch thick

- ◆ To prepare the butter, place the chiles on a rack in a broiler pan.

- ◆ Roast until lightly blackened on all sides, turning frequently. Place the peppers in a brown paper bag and seal tightly.

- ◆ Let stand until cool.

- ◆ Peel, seed and finely chop the chiles.

- ◆ Toss the garlic with the olive oil in a bowl. Place in a small baking pan or garlic roaster.

- ◆ Bake, covered, at 400 degrees for 30 minutes. Let stand until cool.

- ◆ Remove the garlic from the baking pan, reserving the olive oil. Peel the garlic and mash.

- ◆ Mix the butter, chili powder and Tabasco sauce in a bowl. Stir in the chiles and reserved oil. Add the mashed garlic and mix well.

- ◆ To prepare the steaks, grill the steaks over hot coals until of the desired degree of doneness. Remove to individual dinner plates.

- ◆ Top each steak with the desired amount of Garlic and Chili Butter. Serve the remaining butter as a spread for toasted bread slices.

Note:
Avoid contact with your eyes when working with hot peppers.

 Italian Meatballs

Serves 6 to 8

2 pounds ground round

1 medium onion, finely chopped

2 eggs, beaten or equivalent
amount of egg substitute

1/2 cup grated Parmesan cheese
(optional)

1/2 cup seasoned bread crumbs

1/3 cup vegetable broth

1/4 cup parsley flakes

4 to 6 cloves of garlic, crushed

1 teaspoon salt

1 teaspoon freshly cracked
pepper

1/2 teaspoon oregano

1/2 teaspoon basil

◆ Combine the ground round, onion, eggs, cheese, bread crumbs, broth, parsley flakes, garlic, salt, pepper, oregano and basil in a bowl and mix well.

◆ Shape into meatballs of the desired size.

◆ Sauté in a skillet until brown on all sides or add to your favorite tomato sauce recipe to slowly cook.

Note:
Shape the meatballs with your hands. Just wear rubber gloves. It works!

Spaghetti Meat Sauce

Serves 6 to 8

2 medium onions, chopped

4 to 6 cloves of garlic, chopped

2 tablespoons olive oil

2 pounds ground round

1 pound Italian sausage, sliced (optional)

1 pound fresh mushrooms, sliced

2 (12-ounce) cans whole or crushed tomatoes, chopped

2 (12-ounce) cans tomato paste

1½ cups water

6 tablespoons parsley flakes

4 teaspoons sugar

1 tablespoon oregano

1 tablespoon marjoram

2 teaspoons pepper

2 teaspoons basil

1½ teaspoons salt

½ cup grated Romano cheese (optional)

⅓ cup red wine (optional)

hot cooked spaghetti

◆ Sauté the onions and garlic in the olive oil in a stockpot until brown. Remove to a bowl with a slotted spoon, reserving the pan drippings.

◆ Add the ground round and sausage to the reserved pan drippings.

◆ Cook until the ground round is brown and crumbly, stirring constantly; drain. Add the onion mixture and mushrooms and mix well.

◆ Cook for 3 minutes, stirring constantly. Stir in the undrained tomatoes and tomato paste.

◆ Stir in the water, parsley flakes, sugar, oregano, marjoram, pepper, basil and salt and mix well. Bring to a gentle boil; reduce heat.

◆ Simmer, covered, for 2 hours, stirring occasionally. Add additional water if needed. The longer the cooking process the tastier the meat sauce.

◆ Stir in the cheese and red wine.

◆ Cook for 20 minutes longer, stirring occasionally.

◆ Spoon over hot cooked spaghetti.

Note:
Cook for an additional 30 minutes if adding uncooked meatballs.

Sweetbreads with Cream Wine Sauce   Serves 4 to 6

3 pounds sweetbreads

4 cups water

2 tablespoons lemon juice

1 teaspoon salt

$^1/_3$ cup flour

1 teaspoon freshly ground
   pepper

1 cup thinly sliced onion

3 tablespoons olive oil

1 cup sliced mushrooms

$^1/_2$ cup white wine

1 cup half-and-half

1 teaspoon butter, softened
   (optional)

1 teaspoon flour (optional)

$^1/_4$ cup minced fresh parsley

◆ Soak the sweetbreads in enough ice water to cover in a bowl for 2 hours, changing the water several times; drain.

◆ Combine the sweetbreads, 4 cups water, lemon juice and salt in a saucepan.

◆ Simmer for 15 minutes. Remove the sweetbreads and plunge into ice water in a bowl; drain. Remove the membrane that covers the sweetbreads.

◆ Place the sweetbreads in a shallow dish. Cover with a sheet of waxed paper. Place a heavy weight on top of the waxed paper; the sweetbreads will flatten and have a firm shape.

◆ Chill for 3 to 4 hours. Coat the sweetbreads with a mixture of $^1/_3$ cup flour and pepper.

◆ Sauté the onion in the olive oil in a skillet until tender. Stir in the sweetbreads.

◆ Sauté for 3 minutes per side or until golden brown. Remove the sweetbread mixture to a bowl with a slotted spoon, reserving the pan drippings.

◆ Sauté the mushrooms in the reserved pan drippings for 5 minutes. Remove the mushrooms with a slotted spoon to a bowl, reserving the pan drippings.

◆ Deglaze with the white wine. Stir in the half-and-half; do not boil. Add the sweetbread mixture and mushrooms and mix well.

◆ Simmer for 15 minutes, stirring frequently.

◆ Add the butter and 1 teaspoon flour if a thicker consistency is desired.

◆ Sprinkle with the parsley.

Red Wine Mushroom Ragout

Serves 6 to 8

¹/₄ cup vegetable oil

5 pounds meaty beef neck bones, cut into 2-inch pieces

1 pound onions, sliced

7 cups water

2 (750-milliliter) bottles dry red wine

2 large plum tomatoes, chopped

4 cloves of garlic, chopped

1 teaspoon freshly cracked pepper

¹/₈ teaspoon ground cloves

1 cup chopped shallots

¹/₄ cup unsalted margarine

3 pounds mixed fresh mushrooms, sliced

1 sprig of fresh rosemary

◆ Heat the oil in a heavy saucepan. Add the bones and onions.

◆ Cook for 25 minutes, stirring frequently. Stir in 2 cups of the water.

◆ Cook for 10 minutes, stirring frequently.

◆ Add the remaining 5 cups of water, red wine, tomatoes, garlic, pepper and cloves and mix well. Bring to a boil; reduce heat.

◆ Simmer for 4 hours, stirring occasionally. Add additional water if needed for a thinner consistency. Strain into a bowl, discarding the bones, onions and tomatoes.

◆ Chill, covered, in the refrigerator.

◆ Sauté the shallots in the margarine in a saucepan until tender. Add the mushrooms and rosemary sprig and mix well.

◆ Sauté for 20 to 30 minutes or until the mushrooms are tender. Stir in the chilled stock.

◆ Cook for 5 minutes or until heated through, stirring occasionally.

Note:

This is a wonderfully rich and bold sauce for grilled steak or for beef roasts.

Veal and Artichokes

Serves 4 to 6

2 pounds veal, cut into ³/₄-inch slices

1 teaspoon nutmeg

salt and freshly cracked pepper to taste

¹/₄ cup olive oil

2 cups sliced mushrooms

2 cups sliced fresh steamed, frozen or canned artichoke hearts

¹/₂ cup sliced scallions

1 teaspoon chopped fresh thyme

¹/₂ teaspoon chopped fresh rosemary

1 cup chicken broth

¹/₂ cup vegetable broth

¹/₂ cup white wine

1 cup light sour cream

¹/₂ cup chopped fresh parsley

- ◆ Pound the veal between sheets of waxed paper to flatten. Season both sides with nutmeg, salt and pepper.

- ◆ Sauté the veal in the olive oil in a skillet until cooked through. Remove to a platter with a slotted spoon, reserving the pan drippings. Cover to keep warm.

- ◆ Stir the mushrooms, artichokes and scallions into the reserved pan drippings.

- ◆ Sauté for 3 to 5 minutes. Stir in the thyme and rosemary. Add the chicken broth, vegetable broth and white wine and mix well.

- ◆ Cook until thickened, stirring constantly. Stir in the sour cream gradually.

- ◆ Return the veal to the skillet, spooning the sauce over the veal to cover. Sprinkle with the parsley.

- ◆ Simmer for 5 minutes longer.

 # Veal in Sour Cream

Serves 6

3 medium onions, finely
  chopped

$1/4$ cup olive oil

3 pounds veal, cut into cubes

$3/4$ cup water

1 teaspoon dillweed

salt and freshly ground pepper
  to taste

$1^1/2$ cups sour cream

$1/3$ cup flour

$1/4$ cup chopped fresh parsley

$1^1/2$ teaspoons paprika

hot cooked rice or noodles

◆ Sauté the onions in the olive oil in a skillet until light brown. Add the veal and mix well.

◆ Cook over low heat until brown on all sides. Stir in the water, dillweed, salt and pepper.

◆ Simmer, covered, for 1 hour or until the veal is tender, stirring occasionally.

◆ Stir the flour gradually into the sour cream in a bowl. Add to the skillet and mix well. Taste and adjust seasonings.

◆ Cook just until heated through, stirring occasionally; do no boil.

◆ Remove the veal and sauce to a serving platter. Sprinkle with the parsley and paprika.

◆ Serve with rice or noodles.

 # Osso Bucco

Serves 6

6 veal shanks

flour

1/4 cup (or less) butter,
    margarine or olive oil

1 cup finely chopped celery

1 cup finely chopped onion

1 cup finely chopped carrot

1 pint mushrooms, minced

2 large tomatoes, peeled, seeded,
    chopped

2 teaspoons oregano

2 teaspoons rosemary

2 teaspoons sage

1 teaspoon freshly cracked
    pepper

3 cups white wine

Grated peel of 1 large lemon

1/4 cup chopped fresh parsley

2 anchovy fillets, mashed
    (optional)

4 cloves of garlic, minced

◆ Coat the veal shanks with the flour.

◆ Brown the veal on all sides in the butter in a skillet over high heat. Stir in the celery, onion, carrot, mushrooms, tomatoes, oregano, rosemary, sage and pepper.

◆ Cook, covered, over medium-high heat for 10 minutes, stirring occasionally. Stir in the white wine. Transfer the mixture to a larger skillet if the wine covers the veal.

◆ Simmer, covered, for 2 1/2 hours, stirring occasionally.

◆ Stir in the lemon peel, parsley, anchovies and garlic.

Note:
Serve with rice flavored with chopped onion and cooked in chicken broth.

Chicken and Dumplings

Serves 6 to 8

For the Chicken

1 (4- to 5-pound) hen, cut up

1 tablespoon salt

1 rib celery, sliced

1 lemon, sliced

1 onion, sliced

8 peppercorns

1 bay leaf

For the Dumplings

2 cups flour

2 teaspoons baking powder

1 teaspoon salt

$1/3$ cup vegetable shortening

$1/2$ cup milk

1 egg

- ◆ To prepare the chicken, combine the hen and salt with enough water to cover in a stockpot. Bring to a boil.

- ◆ Add the celery, lemon, onion, peppercorns and bay leaf.

- ◆ Boil for 10 minutes; reduce heat. Skim the surface.

- ◆ Simmer for 2 hours or until the chicken is tender, adding additional water as needed.

- ◆ To prepare the dumplings, combine the flour, baking powder and salt in a bowl.

- ◆ Cut in the shortening until crumbly.

- ◆ Whisk the milk and egg together in a bowl. Add to the crumb mixture, stirring until a firm dough forms. Add additional flour if needed for a firm consistency.

- ◆ Roll the dough $1/4$ inch thick on a lightly floured surface. Cut into strips.

- ◆ Drop the dough strips into the hot broth in the stockpot.

- ◆ Simmer, covered, for 30 minutes. Discard the bay leaf.

Chicken Cacciatore

Serves 6

1 (4-to 5-pound) roasting
   chicken, cut up

salt and pepper to taste

flour

6 tablespoons olive oil

1 pound mushrooms, sliced

1 large onion, chopped

4 cloves of garlic, smashed,
   chopped

1 (16-ounce) can crushed Italian
   tomatoes

$1/2$ cup white wine

1 cup chopped fresh parsley

2 tablespoons thyme

- Sprinkle the chicken with salt and pepper and coat with flour.

- Fry in the olive oil in a skillet until golden brown on all sides.

- Remove the chicken with a slotted spoon to a platter, reserving the pan drippings.

- Stir the mushrooms, onion and garlic into the reserved pan drippings.

- Cook until light brown, stirring frequently. Add the tomatoes and white wine and mix well.

- Cook for 5 minutes, stirring occasionally. Return the chicken to the skillet. Stir in the parsley and thyme.

- Cook, covered, over low heat for 45 minutes or until the chicken is tender, stirring occasionally.

Note:
Delicious served over rice.

Chicken Smothered with Onions   Serves 4

1 (3¹/₂-to 3³/₄-pound) chicken,
    cut into quarters

salt and freshly ground pepper
    to taste

paprika to taste

3 tablespoons olive oil

2 large onions, sliced

³/₄ cup dry white wine

2 bay leaves

1 (15-ounce) can chicken broth

3 tablespoons flour

3 tablespoons water

¹/₄ cup evaporated skim milk

chopped fresh parsley

Garlic Mashed Potatoes
    (page 102)

◆ Sprinkle both sides of the chicken with salt, pepper and paprika.

◆ Cook the chicken in the olive oil in a skillet for 10 minutes or just until light brown on all sides, turning occasionally. Remove with a slotted spoon to a platter, reserving the pan drippings. Cover to keep warm.

◆ Add the onions to the reserved pan drippings, scraping the skillet to loosen any browned bits.

◆ Cook, covered, over low heat for 15 minutes or until tender, stirring occasionally. Arrange the chicken over the onions. Add the white wine and bay leaves. Bring to a boil.

◆ Boil for 8 minutes or until most of the wine has been absorbed and the mixture is of a syrupy consistency, stirring frequently. Stir in the broth.

◆ Bring to a boil; reduce heat.

◆ Simmer, covered, for 30 minutes or until the chicken is cooked through, turning occasionally. Transfer the chicken to a platter with a slotted spoon, reserving the pan drippings. Tent with foil to keep warm.

◆ Combine the flour and water in a bowl and mix well. Stir into the reserved pan drippings. Add the evaporated skim milk and mix well.

◆ Simmer for 8 minutes or until thickened and of a sauce consistency, stirring frequently. Return the chicken to the skillet.

◆ Simmer just until heated through, stirring occasionally. Discard the bay leaves. Taste and adjust seasonings.

◆ Spoon Garlic Mashed Potatoes onto 4 dinner plates. Place 1 chicken quarter over each serving of potatoes. Drizzle with the sauce and sprinkle with parsley.

Spiced Roasted Chicken

Serves 4

1 (3- to 4-pound) chicken, cut into quarters

2 tablespoons cinnamon

1 tablespoon nutmeg

salt and freshly ground pepper to taste

2 tablespoons olive oil

2 large onions, cut into quarters

6 cloves of garlic, mashed

2 yellow bell peppers, cut into quarters

2 carrots, sliced

1 pint mushrooms, cut into quarters

2 tomatoes, peeled, seeded, cut into quarters

2 cups torn corn tortillas

- ◆ Rub the chicken with a mixture of the cinnamon, nutmeg, salt and pepper.

- ◆ Brown the chicken on all sides in an ovenproof skillet sprayed with nonstick olive oil cooking spray for 15 minutes, turning frequently. Remove to a platter with a slotted spoon. Cover to keep warm.

- ◆ Heat the olive oil in the same skillet until hot. Add the onions and garlic.

- ◆ Sauté until tender. Stir in the bell peppers, carrots, mushrooms and tomatoes.

- ◆ Sauté for 6 to 8 minutes or until tender; do not overcook. Add the tortillas and mix well. Return the chicken to the skillet.

- ◆ Bake, covered, at 350 degrees for 30 minutes or until the chicken is cooked through.

 Apricot Chicken

Serves 6

2¹/₂ to 3 pounds chicken breasts
1 teaspoon ginger
salt and pepper to taste
1¹/₂ cups orange marmalade
¹/₃ cup apple juice
¹/₃ cup orange juice
1 cup dried apricots
1 cup golden raisins
¹/₄ cup packed brown sugar

- ◆ Arrange the chicken in a single layer in a 9x13-inch baking dish.
- ◆ Sprinkle with the ginger, salt and pepper.
- ◆ Spread the marmalade over the chicken. Pour the apple juice and orange juice over the top.
- ◆ Bake at 375 degrees for 20 minutes.
- ◆ Add the apricots and raisins. Sprinkle with the brown sugar. Baste with the pan drippings.
- ◆ Bake, covered, for 40 to 45 minutes or until the chicken is cooked through.

Note:
If the pan drippings are thin and watery, uncover and bake for 20 minutes longer.

Chicken Stuffed with Spinach and Cheese

Serves 6

For the Spinach and Cheese Filling

8 ounces fresh spinach, trimmed

1 cup ricotta cheese

1 egg or equivalent amount of egg substitute

1/3 cup grated Parmesan cheese

1/4 cup snipped fresh chives

2 tablespoons chopped garlic

2 teaspoons freshly cracked pepper

For the Chicken

6 chicken breast halves

2 tablespoons olive oil

1/2 teaspoon oregano

1/2 teaspoon thyme

1/2 teaspoon rosemary

1/2 teaspoon salt (optional)

- ◆ To prepare the filling, rinse the spinach; do not pat dry.

- ◆ Cook, covered, in a saucepan for 3 to 4 minutes or until tender. Cool slightly.

- ◆ Squeeze the moisture from the spinach.

- ◆ Process in a blender or food processor until finely chopped.

- ◆ Combine the ricotta cheese, egg, Parmesan cheese, chives, garlic and pepper in a bowl and mix well. Stir in the spinach.

- ◆ To prepare the chicken, place the chicken skin side up on a hard surface. Press down with the palm of your hand to pop the bones to allow the chicken to lie flat.

- ◆ Loosen the skin covering the chicken breast to form a pocket, making sure not to tear the skin.

- ◆ Place the chicken skin side up in a shallow roasting pan. Stuff each pocket with some of the filling.

- ◆ Brush the chicken with the olive oil. Sprinkle with the oregano, thyme, rosemary and salt.

- ◆ Roast at 375 degrees for 35 to 45 minutes or until the chicken is cooked through and the skin is crisp and brown.

- ◆ Serve hot or at room temperature.

Garlic Lovers' Chicken Breasts with Olives

Serves 2 to 4

spinach linguini

¹/₃ cup smashed sliced garlic

¹/₄ cup olive oil

4 boneless chicken breast halves

salt and freshly cracked pepper
   to taste

1 large tomato, peeled, seeded,
   chopped

1 yellow bell pepper, roasted,
   peeled, sliced

10 large green olives, sliced

¹/₂ cup rolled sliced fresh basil

1 cup grated Parmesan cheese

- ◆ Prepare the linguini using package directions; drain. Cover to keep warm.

- ◆ Sauté the garlic in the olive oil in a skillet until golden brown. Remove to a bowl using a slotted spoon, reserving the pan drippings.

- ◆ Sprinkle the chicken lightly with salt and pepper.

- ◆ Sauté the chicken in the reserved pan drippings until brown and thoroughly cooked. Remove the chicken to a platter with a slotted spoon, reserving the pan drippings. Cover to keep warm.

- ◆ Add the garlic, tomato, yellow pepper, olives and basil to the reserved pan drippings and mix well.

- ◆ Cook just until heated through, stirring constantly.

- ◆ Arrange the linguini on dinner plates. Top each serving with 1 or 2 chicken breasts. Spoon the tomato and olive sauce over the chicken. Sprinkle generously with the cheese.

Herb-Marinated Chicken Breasts   Serves 12

12 boneless skinless chicken
   breast halves

2 bottles Italian salad dressing
   (regular, light or fat-free)

1/2 cup parsley flakes

2 tablespoons granulated garlic

2 tablespoons all-purpose Greek
   seasoning/salt-free

2 tablespoons freshly ground
   peppercorns

1 tablespoon dried rosemary

1 tablespoon dried basil

1 tablespoon dried thyme

1 tablespoon dried marjoram

1 tablespoon Beau Monde
   seasoning

- ◆ Arrange the chicken in a large dish with high sides.

- ◆ Combine the salad dressing, parsley flakes, garlic, multi-Greek seasoning, peppercorns, rosemary, basil, thyme, marjoram and Beau Monde seasoning in a bowl and mix well. Pour over the chicken, turning to coat.

- ◆ Marinate, covered, in the refrigerator for 1 to 3 days, turning twice daily. The longer the marinating time the more tender and tastier the chicken.

- ◆ Grill over hot coals for 7 to 9 minutes per side or until cooked through.

- ◆ Note: Grill an additional 2 minutes per side if using chicken breasts with skin and bone.

- ◆ Serve hot or at room temperature.

Note:
Delicious served over mixed salad greens.

Pan-Seared Chicken with Ratatouille   Serves 4

1 teaspoon freshly cracked
   pepper

4 chicken breasts halves

2 tablespoons olive oil

2 medium onions, sliced

1 medium yellow bell pepper,
   sliced

1 medium zucchini, sliced

1 small eggplant, peeled,
   chopped

1 cup mushrooms, cut into
   quarters

3 cloves of garlic, chopped

4 tomatoes, peeled, seeded,
   chopped

1/4 cup mixed dried herbs
   (Anne Katrin's Greek Herb
   mix, basil, thyme, rosemary
   and oregano)

1/4 cup Kalamata olive halves

1/2 cup grated Parmesan cheese

◆ Press the pepper into the top of the chicken breasts.

◆ Sear the chicken in a skillet sprayed with nonstick cooking spray over high heat for 3 minutes per side. Remove to a platter. Cover with foil to keep warm.

◆ Add the olive oil to the skillet. Add the onions.

◆ Sauté over medium heat for 3 minutes. Stir in the yellow pepper, zucchini, eggplant, mushrooms and garlic.

◆ Sauté for 8 to 10 minutes. Add the tomatoes and mixed herbs and mix well.

◆ Simmer, covered, until all of the liquid is absorbed, stirring occasionally. Remove from heat. Stir in the olives. Return the chicken to the skillet.

◆ Cook, covered, for 10 minutes or until the chicken is cooked through, stirring occasionally.

◆ Serve with the Parmesan cheese.

Note:
May use boneless skinless chicken breasts.

Garlic Chicken with Spinach and Cilantro

Serves 6

2 pounds boneless skinless
chicken breasts, thinly sliced

1/2 cup chopped scallion bulbs

5 cloves of garlic, chopped

3 tablespoons chopped peeled
gingerroot

1/3 cup low-sodium soy sauce

1 teaspoon red pepper flakes

2 tablespoons olive oil

1/2 cup (about) chicken broth

1/3 cup red wine vinegar

1 cup chopped fresh cilantro

1/2 cup chopped whole scallions

1/4 cup rice wine vinegar

2 tablespoons Dijon mustard

2 tablespoons olive oil

freshly ground pepper to taste

1 pound fresh spinach, trimmed,
chopped

Bibb lettuce, radicchio or red
cabbage cups

◆ Combine the chicken, 1/2 cup chopped scallion
bulbs, garlic, gingerroot, 2 tablespoons of the soy
sauce and red pepper flakes in a bowl and mix well.

◆ Heat 2 tablespoons olive oil in a skillet until hot but
not smoking. Add the chicken mixture.

◆ Stir-fry over medium heat until the chicken is light
brown. Increase heat to high.

◆ Stir in the remaining soy sauce, broth and red
wine vinegar.

◆ Cook until the mixture begins to thicken, stirring
constantly. Remove from heat. Stir in the cilantro
and 1/2 cup chopped whole scallions.

◆ Combine the rice wine vinegar, Dijon mustard,
2 tablespoons olive oil and pepper in a bowl and
mix well. Pour over the spinach in a bowl, tossing to
coat. Add to the chicken mixture and mix well.

◆ Spoon into lettuce or red cabbage cups.

 Chicken and Rice Casserole

Serves 6 to 8

1 cup sliced carrots

2 large onions, chopped

1 cup sliced mushrooms

3 tablespoons vegetable oil

4 cups chopped cooked chicken

1 cup coarsely chopped celery

1 cup sliced marinated artichoke hearts

1/4 cup chopped fresh parsley

2 tablespoons all purpose Greek seasoning/salt-free

1 tablespoon cracked pepper

2 cups uncooked basmati rice

2 cups chicken broth

◆ Blanch the carrots in a small amount of water in a saucepan. Drain, reserving 1 cup of the liquid.

◆ Sauté the onions and mushrooms in the oil in a skillet until tender.

◆ Combine the carrots, onion mixture, chicken, celery, artichokes, parsley, Greek seasoning and pepper in a bowl and mix well.

◆ Spread the rice in a 9x13-inch baking dish sprayed with nonstick cooking spray. Spoon the chicken mixture over the rice. Pour a mixture of the reserved carrot liquid and broth over the top.

◆ Bake, covered, at 350 degrees for 30 to 40 minutes, adding additional broth as needed. Remove the cover during the last 10 minutes of the cooking process.

Cornish Game Hens with Rice

Serves 6 to 8

3 onions, chopped

¹/₄ cup olive oil

4 Cornish game hens

1¹/₂ cups sweet red wine

2 cups tomato purée

¹/₂ teaspoon grated nutmeg

¹/₂ teaspoon red pepper flakes

1 cinnamon stick

2 cups chicken broth, heated

1¹/₂ cups long grain rice

salt and freshly ground pepper to taste

¹/₂ cup chopped fresh Italian parsley

◆ Sauté the onions in the olive oil in a skillet until tender. Add the game hens.

◆ Cook for 10 to 15 minutes or until brown on all sides, turning frequently. Pour in the red wine.

◆ Simmer for 5 minutes, stirring occasionally. Stir in the tomato purée, nutmeg, red pepper flakes and cinnamon stick. Bring to a gentle boil; reduce heat.

◆ Simmer for 15 to 20 minutes, stirring occasionally.

◆ Combine the rice and broth in a bowl and mix well. Stir into the tomato purée mixture. Season with salt and pepper.

◆ Simmer, covered, for 15 to 20 minutes or until the game hens are cooked through, adding additional broth as needed. Discard the cinnamon stick. Sprinkle with the parsley.

Mushroom and Crawfish Dressing   Serves 10

$^1/_4$ cup margarine

$^1/_4$ cup olive oil

1 large red onion, chopped

$^1/_4$ cup chopped smashed garlic

1 pint mixed wild mushrooms
   (cremini, oyster, portobello),
   sliced

6 scallions, sliced

1$^1/_2$ cups frozen crawfish tails

1 cup medium fresh shrimp,
   peeled, deveined

1 cup seasoned bread crumbs

2 teaspoons all purpose Greek
   seasoning/salt-free

$^1/_2$ teaspoon Creole seasoning

freshly cracked pepper to taste

◆ Heat the margarine and olive oil in a skillet until hot. Add the onion and garlic.

◆ Sauté over high heat until tender. Stir in the mushrooms.

◆ Sauté over medium-high heat for 5 minutes. Add the scallions, crayfish tails, shrimp, bread crumbs, Greek seasoning, Creole seasoning and pepper, stirring until mixed.

◆ Use as a stuffing for poultry or wild fowl.

 Oyster and Pecan Dressing

Serves 10

8 ounces turkey sausage, sliced

½ cup butter

1 cup chopped onion

1 cup chopped celery

6 cups dry bread cubes

3 cups drained fresh oysters

1 cup coarsely chopped pecans

¼ cup chopped fresh parsley

1½ teaspoons Worcestershire sauce

1 teaspoon salt

¼ teaspoon freshly ground pepper

- Sauté the sausage in a 6-quart Dutch oven for 5 minutes or until golden brown. Remove the sausage to a bowl with a slotted spoon, reserving the pan drippings.

- Heat the butter with the reserved pan drippings until the butter melts. Add the onion and celery.

- Sauté for 5 minutes or until the onion is golden brown. Remove from heat.

- Add the bread cubes, oysters, pecans, parsley, Worcestershire sauce, salt and pepper and toss lightly.

- Use as a stuffing for poultry.

 Bouillabaisse   *Serves 6 to 8*

1 pound snapper, flounder or
   halibut fillets

1 pound sea bass, sole or
   mackerel fillets

2 (8-ounce) lobster tails

1 pound fresh crab meat

1 pound clams in shells

1 pound mussels in shells

2 cups fresh oysters with liquor

8 ounces scallops

2 (10-ounce) cans vegetable
   broth

1 fennel bulb, coarsely chopped

2 large tomatoes, chopped

1½ cups chopped onions

6 large cloves of garlic, crushed

¼ cup olive oil

¼ cup flour

1 large can crushed tomatoes

2 teaspoons salt

2 teaspoons ground basil

1 teaspoon ground thyme

1 teaspoon red pepper flakes

¼ teaspoon saffron

1 bay leaf

freshly ground pepper to taste

2 lemons, sliced

6 to 8 slices French bread

Aioli Sauce (page 92)

freshly chopped parsley

◆ Combine the snapper, sea bass, lobster tails, crab meat, clams and mussels with enough water to cover in a stockpot. Bring to a boil; reduce heat.

◆ Simmer until the fish flakes easily, stirring occasionally. Add the oysters and scallops.

◆ Cook for 5 minutes longer. Drain, reserving the liquid.

◆ Remove the lobster meat from the shell. Place the lobster and shell with the snapper, sea bass, crab meat, clams, mussels, oysters and scallops on a serving platter. Cover to keep warm.

◆ Combine the reserved liquid and vegetable broth with enough water to measure 10 cups.

◆ Sauté the fennel, 2 tomatoes, onions and garlic in the olive oil in a Dutch oven until tender. Stir in the flour.

◆ Cook over low heat until mixed. Remove from heat. Whisk in the reserved liquid and broth mixture.

◆ Cook until smooth and bubbly, stirring constantly. Stir in the undrained canned tomatoes, salt, basil, thyme, red pepper flakes, saffron, bay leaf and pepper. Bring to a boil; reduce heat.

◆ Simmer for 15 to 20 minutes or until the mixture is of the consistency of soup. Taste and adjust seasonings. Discard the bay leaf. Stir in the lemon slices.

◆ To assemble, spread each bread slice with some of the Aioli sauce.

◆ Place 1 bread slice in each soup bowl. Ladle the soup over the bread.

◆ Sprinkle the seafood with parsley and serve with the soup; each guest adds the desired amount of seafood to their serving.

◆ Serve with the remaining Aioli Sauce.

Grouper and Shrimp with Tomatoes   Serves 4

2 cups sliced onions

6 cloves of garlic, sliced

1/4 cup olive oil

6 (red and yellow) tomatoes, seeded, coarsely chopped

1 tablespoon ground pepper

1 (14-ounce) can vegetable broth

1/4 cup white wine (optional)

1/4 cup lemon juice

1 pound grouper fillet, cut into 4 portions

1 pound medium shrimp, cooked, peeled, deveined

1 (14-ounce) can artichoke hearts, drained, coarsely chopped

1 cup coarsely chopped fresh basil

1 cup black or green pitted Greek olives

1 cup crumbled feta cheese

◆ Sauté the onions and garlic in the olive oil in a skillet until tender. Add the tomatoes and pepper and mix well.

◆ Sauté for 2 minutes. Remove the tomatoes with a slotted spoon to a bowl, reserving the pan juices.

◆ Stir the broth, white wine and lemon juice into the reserved pan juices. Bring to a simmer. Add the grouper.

◆ Poach for 2 minutes per side. Add the shrimp.

◆ Cook for 1 minute. Remove the grouper and shrimp with a slotted spoon to a serving platter, reserving the pan juices. Cover to keep warm.

◆ Stir the tomatoes, artichokes, basil and olives into the reserved pan juices.

◆ Cook just until the boiling point, stirring frequently. Pour over the fish and shrimp. Sprinkle with the feta cheese.

◆ Serve immediately.

Mediterranean Seared Fish with Garlic and Basil Pasta

Serves 4

1 pound grouper, amberjack, sea
  bass or salmon fillet, skin
  removed

freshly ground pepper to taste

2 to 4 tablespoons olive oil

1/4 cup low-sodium soy sauce

1 package fettuccini, cooked
  al dente, drained

1/3 cup basil pesto

olive oil to taste

1 pound portobello mushrooms,
  julienned

3 cloves of garlic, chopped

1 bunch fresh asparagus,
  steamed or poached, cut into
  1-inch pieces

4 Roma tomatoes, seeded,
  chopped

white balsamic vinegar to taste

1/2 cup julienned fresh basil

freshly grated Parmesan cheese

◆ Cut the grouper into 1/2-inch cubes. Sprinkle
  with pepper.

◆ Drizzle 2 to 4 tablespoons olive oil on a griddle.
  Heat until hot; do not allow to smoke. Drizzle with
  the soy sauce. Arrange the grouper in a single layer
  on the hot griddle.

◆ Fry until the grouper is brown and slightly crusty on
  both sides and flakes easily; do not burn. Remove to
  a platter. Cover to keep warm.

◆ Combine the pasta, basil pesto and desired amount
  of olive oil in a bowl, tossing to coat.

◆ Sauté the mushrooms and garlic in a sauté pan
  sprayed with nonstick olive oil cooking spray over
  medium-high heat for 3 minutes. Add to the pasta
  mixture and mix gently.

◆ Mix in the asparagus and tomatoes. Sprinkle with
  the balsamic vinegar and toss gently. Taste and add
  additional olive oil and balsamic vinegar if desired.

◆ Divide the pasta mixture evenly among 4 dinner
  plates. Top each serving with 1/4 of the grouper.
  Sprinkle with the basil and cheese.

Pecan-Crusted Mahi Mahi with Mango Salsa

Serves 6

For the Mango Salsa

2 cups chopped mango

1/2 orange or yellow bell pepper, chopped

1/2 red onion, roasted, chopped

1/4 cup chopped fresh cilantro

1 teaspoon chopped chives

Juice of 1 lime

salt to taste

For the Mahi Mahi

2 tablespoons coriander seeds

2 tablespoons cumin seeds

1 tablespoon peppercorns

2 teaspoons coarse salt

2 pounds Mahi Mahi fillets, skin removed

1/2 cup canola oil

1/2 cup chopped pecans

◆ To prepare the salsa, combine the mango, orange pepper, onion, cilantro, chives, lime juice and salt in a bowl and mix well.

◆ Store, covered, in the refrigerator.

◆ To prepare the fish, process the coriander seeds, cumin seeds, peppercorns and coarse salt in an old coffee grinder until ground.

◆ Brush the fillets with the 1/4 cup of the canola oil. Coat both sides evenly with the seasoning mixture and chopped pecans.

◆ Sear the fillets on both sides in the remaining 1/4 cup canola oil in a sauté pan, turning frequently.

◆ Arrange the fillets in a baking pan.

◆ Bake at 400 degrees for 5 minutes or until the fish flakes easily.

◆ Serve with Mango Salsa.

 # Poached Salmon

Serves 18

20 cups water

2 cups dry white wine

2 cups coarsely chopped onions

1 cup coarsely chopped celery

1 cup coarsely chopped leek
    tops

1 cup loosely packed sprigs of
    parsley

2 carrots, peeled, cut into
    1/4-inch slices

1/3 cup coarsely chopped
    dillweed stems

1/4 cup coarsely chopped shallots
    (optional)

2 bay leaves

10 peppercorns

1 teaspoon dried thyme

1 teaspoon red pepper flakes

salt to taste

1 (7- to 8-pound) salmon with
    head and tail, scaled, fins
    removed

- Fit a fish poacher with a rack.

- Combine the water, white wine, onions, celery, leek tops, parsley, carrots, dillweed, shallots, bay leaves, peppercorns, thyme, red pepper flakes and salt in the poacher and mix well.

- Simmer for 20 to 30 minutes. Remove from heat.

- Let stand in cooking liquid until cool.

- Cut a length of cheesecloth 1 foot longer than the salmon.

- Lay the cheesecloth on a flat surface. Center the fish on the cheesecloth.

- Roll the salmon in the cheesecloth and tie in 3 or 4 locations with kitchen twine.

- Place the salmon in the poacher. Bring to a boil.

- Cook for 10 minutes per inch of thickness at the midsection or until the salmon flakes easily. A salmon weighing 7 to 8 pounds should cook in 20 minutes.

- Lift the rack out and allow to rest on the top of the poacher. Discard the vegetables on the rack.

- Transfer the salmon to a flat surface. Discard the cheesecloth and place on a serving platter.

- Chill, covered, until serving time.

Note:

To avoid overcooking, let the salmon cook in barely simmering liquid for 15 minutes. Remove from heat. Let stand in the liquid for 15 to 20 minutes longer. Tug at the bones along the backbone of the fish where the dorsal fin was removed. If this slips out easily and there are no signs of pink at the base of the small bones, the salmon is cooked through. It is best to have salmon slightly undercooked rather than overcooked.

 # Mustard-Coated Salmon

Serves 6

6 (8-ounce) salmon fillets or
    steaks

1 cup Dijon mustard

$^1/_2$ cup olive oil

1 cup chopped fresh herbs
    (chives, parsley and thyme)

freshly ground pepper to taste

- ◆ Coat the salmon with the Dijon mustard. Seal the mustard coating with a light layer of olive oil.

- ◆ Sprinkle with the fresh herbs. Season heavily with pepper.

- ◆ Chill, covered, for 2 hours or longer.

- ◆ Place the salmon in a shallow baking pan sprayed with nonstick cooking spray.

- ◆ Bake at 350 degrees for 15 to 20 minutes or until the salmon flakes easily.

 Baltimore Crab Cakes

Serves 6

¹/₄ cup butter or margarine

¹/₂ cup flour

2 cups evaporated skim milk

1 egg, beaten or equivalent
amount of egg substitute

¹/₄ cup chopped fresh parsley

1 tablespoon Worcestershire
sauce

1 teaspoon cracked pepper

¹/₂ teaspoon salt

¹/₄ teaspoon dry mustard

2 pounds lump crab meat

1 cup skim milk

1 egg

salt and pepper to taste

unseasoned bread or cracker
crumbs

vegetable oil for frying

- Heat the butter in a skillet until melted. Add the flour, stirring until smooth. Stir in the evaporated skim milk.

- Cook until thickened, stirring constantly.

- Add 1 egg, stirring until blended. Remove from heat.

- Let stand until cool.

- Stir in the parsley, Worcestershire sauce, 1 teaspoon pepper, ¹/₂ teaspoon salt and dry mustard. Add the crab meat and mix well.

- Shape into large patties.

- Chill, covered, for 1 to 2 hours.

- Whisk the skim milk, 1 egg and salt and pepper to taste together in a bowl.

- Dip the patties in the egg mixture. Coat with the bread crumbs.

- Fry in hot oil in a skillet for 15 minutes or until brown on both sides; drain.

 Baked Stuffed Shrimp

Serves 5 to 6

2 pounds shrimp (12 to 15 per pound)

3 tablespoons butter or margarine

1 orange bell pepper, finely chopped

1/3 cup minced onion

2 tablespoons minced shallots or green onions

1 cup soft bread crumbs

1 teaspoon salt

freshly ground pepper to taste

1 egg, beaten

2 tablespoons melted butter or margarine

chopped fresh parsley

◆ Peel and devein 6 of the shrimp.

◆ Sauté the peeled and deveined shrimp in 3 tablespoons butter in a sauté pan until the shrimp turn pink. Remove the shrimp with a slotted spoon and finely chop, reserving the pan drippings.

◆ Stir the orange pepper, onion and shallots into the reserved pan drippings.

◆ Cook for 3 to 4 minutes, stirring frequently. Remove from heat. Stir in the chopped shrimp, bread crumbs, salt and pepper. Mix in the egg.

◆ Peel the remaining shrimp, leaving the tails intact.

◆ Place the shrimp backside down on a hard surface. Make a horizontal slit to but not through to form a pocket. Remove the vein.

◆ Spoon some of the bread crumb mixture into each pocket. Bring the tail over the stuffing.

◆ Arrange the shrimp tails up in a greased shallow baking dish. May store, covered, in the refrigerator at this point until just before baking. Drizzle with 2 tablespoons butter.

◆ Bake at 400 degrees for 10 to 12 minutes. Remove to a heated platter. Sprinkle with parsley.

Curried Shrimp with Apples   Serves 4

1 large Granny Smith apple,
   peeled, sliced

1/3 cup finely chopped onion

2 cloves of garlic, smashed,
   chopped

1/4 cup butter

1/4 cup flour

2 tablespoons curry

1 teaspoon ginger

3 whole cloves

2 cups chicken or vegetable
   broth

3/4 cup cream

1 tablespoon lemon juice

salt to taste

2 pounds medium shrimp

hot cooked rice

- ◆ Sauté the apple, onion and garlic in the butter in a large skillet for 3 minutes. Stir in the flour, curry, ginger and cloves.

- ◆ Add the broth gradually, stirring constantly.

- ◆ Cook until thickened, stirring constantly. Add the cream, lemon juice and salt and mix well.

- ◆ Combine the shrimp with enough water to cover in a saucepan. Bring to a slow boil.

- ◆ Cook for 3 minutes or until the shrimp turn pink; drain. Peel and devein.

- ◆ Add the shrimp to the cream mixture and mix well.

- ◆ Cook just until heated through, stirring frequently; do not over cook.

- ◆ Spoon over hot cooked rice.

Ginger Shrimp with Pea Pods

Serves 4

3 tablespoons vegetable or peanut oil

$\frac{1}{2}$ teaspoon sesame oil, or to taste

1 pound shrimp, peeled, deveined

2 cloves of garlic, crushed, chopped

2 cups fresh or frozen snow peas

1 (8-ounce) can sliced water chestnuts, drained

$\frac{1}{2}$ cup vegetable broth

2 tablespoons lite soy sauce, or to taste

1 tablespoon cornstarch

1 tablespoon cold water

1 tablespoon grated fresh gingerroot

2 to 3 cups hot cooked rice

◆ Heat the vegetable oil and sesame oil in a wok or heavy skillet until hot but not smoking. Add the shrimp.

◆ Stir-fry for 2 minutes. Remove to a platter with a slotted spoon, reserving the pan drippings. Cover to keep warm.

◆ Add the garlic to the reserved pan drippings.

◆ Stir-fry for 15 to 20 seconds. Add the snow peas, water chestnuts, broth and soy sauce and mix well.

◆ Stir-fry for 2 minutes. Add a mixture of the cornstarch and water, stirring until mixed.

◆ Return the shrimp to the wok. Stir in the gingerroot.

◆ Stir-fry until the sauce thickens and the mixture is heated through.

◆ Spoon over hot cooked rice. Serve immediately.

 Cucumber Dill Sauce

Makes 1½ cups

1 cup sour cream
½ cup grated seeded cucumber
1 tablespoon finely chopped
   fresh chives
1 teaspoon dillweed
½ teaspoon salt
½ teaspoon white pepper

◆ Combine the sour cream, cucumber, chives, dillweed salt and white pepper in a bowl and mix well.

◆ Store, covered, in the refrigerator until serving time.

Note:
May be prepared 1 day in advance and stored, covered, in the refrigerator.

 Aioli Sauce

Makes ½ cup

2 egg yolks
3 medium cloves of garlic
1 teaspoon paprika
1 teaspoon fresh lemon juice
¼ teaspoon salt
¼ teaspoon cayenne
¼ cup olive oil

◆ Combine the egg yolks, garlic, paprika, lemon juice, salt and cayenne in a blender container.

◆ Process at High speed for 2 minutes or until the garlic is finely chopped.

◆ Add the olive oil in a fine stream, processing constantly until smooth.

Vegetarian

# Romano-Stuffed Artichokes

Serves 8

2 cups buttered bread crumbs

1 cup grated Romano cheese

1 cup minced fresh parsley

6 cloves of garlic, minced

1 teaspoon freshly cracked
  pepper

salt to taste

4 lemons

8 fresh artichokes

$\frac{1}{2}$ cup olive oil

◆ Combine the bread crumbs, cheese, parsley, garlic, pepper and salt in a bowl and mix well.

◆ Grate the peel of the lemons. Stir into the bread crumb mixture.

◆ Cut a slice from the bottom of each artichoke in order for the artichokes to sit flat.

◆ Trim the leaves. Spread the leaves apart with your fingers. Sprinkle the bread crumb mixture generously over each artichoke until all the spaces are filled.

◆ Squeeze the juice from 2 of the lemons into a bowl. Stir in the olive oil.

◆ Drizzle the olive oil mixture over the artichokes.

◆ Place the artichokes on a rack in a roasting pan. Add water to measure 1 inch.

◆ Bake, covered with foil, at 350 degrees for 50 to 60 minutes or until tender. Test for doneness by removing a leaf near the center.

 Baked Beans   Serves 12

3 (20-ounce) cans pork and
  beans

1 pound sharp Cheddar cheese,
  cubed

1 can applesauce

1 can tomato sauce

2 large onions, chopped

1 bunch green onions, chopped

1 yellow bell pepper, chopped

1 red bell pepper, chopped

1 orange bell pepper, chopped

6 ribs celery, finely chopped

3/4 cup tomato juice

1/2 cup packed brown sugar

2 tablespoons (heaping)
  prepared mustard

salt and pepper to taste

◆ Combine the pork and beans, cheese, applesauce,
  tomato sauce, onions, green onions, bell peppers,
  celery, tomato juice, brown sugar, prepared mustard,
  salt and pepper in a bowl and mix well.

◆ Spoon into a large baking pan.

◆ Bake, covered, at 300 degrees for 4 hours. Add water
  in small quantities during the cooking process if the
  beans become dry.

Note:
May substitute 2 large chopped peeled apples for the
applesauce.

 # Broccoli Frittata

Serves 6 to 8

4 cups broccoli florets

8 eggs or equivalent amount of egg substitute

1 cup grated Parmesan cheese

1/2 cup milk or evaporated skim milk

1/2 teaspoon grated nutmeg

salt and pepper to taste

1/4 cup butter or margarine

◆ Blanch the broccoli in boiling water in a saucepan for 3 to 5 minutes or until tender-crisp.

◆ Rinse and drain. Let stand until cool.

◆ Beat the eggs, cheese, milk, nutmeg, salt and pepper in a bowl until mixed. Stir in the broccoli.

◆ Heat the butter in a 12-inch ovenproof skillet over medium heat until melted. Pour in the broccoli mixture, tilting the skillet to spread evenly.

◆ Cook over low heat until set.

◆ Broil until brown. Cut into wedges.

◆ Serve immediately.

Brussels Sprouts with Poppy Seeds

Serves 8

2 pounds large brussels sprouts
Juice of 1 lemon
¹/₄ cup olive oil
4 cloves of garlic, chopped
2 tablespoons poppy seeds
¹/₂ cup white wine
salt and freshly ground pepper to taste

- ◆ Cut the stems from the brussels sprouts. Cut lengthwise into halves.

- ◆ Cut each half into ¹/₈-inch slices.

- ◆ Combine the brussels sprouts and lemon juice in a bowl, tossing to coat.

- ◆ Heat the olive oil in a sauté pan just to the smoking point. Stir in the brussels sprouts, garlic and poppy seeds.

- ◆ Mix in the white wine.

- ◆ Cook for 3 minutes, stirring constantly. The brussels sprouts should be bright green and barely crunchy.

- ◆ Reduce the heat to low. Season with salt and pepper.

- ◆ Cook for 1 minute, stirring frequently.

- ◆ Serve immediately.

 Carrot Soufflé

Serves 10 to 12

2 (16-ounce) packages frozen
  carrots
1³/₄ cups sugar
1 (12-ounce) can evaporated
  skim milk
1 cup melted margarine
³/₄ cup flour
4 eggs
1 tablespoon vanilla extract

- ◆ Cook the carrots using package directions; drain.
- ◆ Process the carrots in a food processor until creamy.
- ◆ Let stand until cool.
- ◆ Add the sugar, skim milk, margarine, flour, eggs and vanilla.
- ◆ Process until mixed.
- ◆ Pour the carrot mixture into a 9x13-inch baking dish or 2-quart soufflé dish sprayed with nonstick cooking spray.
- ◆ Bake at 350 degrees for 30 minutes.
- ◆ Increase the oven temperature to 400 degrees.
- ◆ Bake for 30 to 50 minutes longer or until brown.

 # Cauliflower Stroganoff

Serves 6

1 head cauliflower, trimmed
4 cups vegetable stock
2 onions, finely chopped
2 cloves of garlic, crushed
2 tablespoons brown sugar
2 tablespoons paprika
1 tablespoon chopped fresh
   thyme
salt and pepper to taste
1 cup light sour cream
1/4 cup Cognac (optional)
1 tablespoon cider vinegar
2 tablespoons cornstarch
1/4 cup cold water

- ◆ Combine the whole cauliflower head and stock in a steamer or saucepan.
- ◆ Steam or boil until tender-crisp. Drain, reserving 2 cups of the liquid.
- ◆ Let stand until cool.
- ◆ Sauté the onions and garlic in a nonstick skillet until tender. Stir in the brown sugar, paprika, thyme, salt and pepper. Add the reserved liquid, sour cream, Cognac and vinegar and mix well.
- ◆ Combine the cornstarch and cold water in a bowl and mix well. Stir into the sour cream mixture.
- ◆ Cook until thickened or of a sauce consistency, stirring constantly.
- ◆ Place the cauliflower head in a round baking pan. Pour the sauce over the top.
- ◆ Bake at 350 degrees for 15 minutes.
- ◆ Serve hot or cold.

Stuffed Eggplant with Tomatoes and Onions

Serves 8

4 medium eggplant

olive oil for frying

4 large onions, sliced

1/2 cup olive oil

1 yellow bell pepper, julienned

4 cloves of garlic, minced

1/2 teaspoon red pepper flakes

1 1/2 cups chopped peeled fresh
   tomatoes

1 cup chopped Italian parsley

1/4 cup thinly sliced basil leaves

2 cups grated pecorino cheese

salt and freshly cracked pepper
   to taste

8 slices tomato

1 cup bread crumbs

olive oil to taste

- Cut the eggplant lengthwise into halves.

- Sauté in 1/4 cup of the olive oil in a skillet until golden brown on all sides sides; drain.

- Sauté the onions in the remaining 1/4 cup olive in a skillet until tender. Stir in the yellow pepper, garlic and red pepper flakes.

- Sauté for 3 to 5 minutes. Stir in the chopped tomatoes.

- Cook over high heat until the liquid is absorbed, stirring constantly. Stir in the parsley and basil. Remove from heat.

- Let stand until cool.

- Scoop 3 to 4 tablespoons of the eggplant pulp from each half to form a shell, reserving the pulp. Arrange the shells on a baking sheet sprayed with nonstick cooking spray.

- Chop the reserved pulp and stir into the tomato mixture. Add the cheese and mix well. Season with salt and pepper.

- Spoon the tomato mixture into the eggplant shells. Top with a tomato slice and sprinkle with bread crumbs. Drizzle or spray with olive oil to taste.

- Bake at 375 degrees for 35 to 45 minutes or until tender.

- Serve warm or at room temperature.

 # Onion Tart

Serves 6

6 large yellow onions, thinly sliced

3 tablespoons olive oil

3 tablespoons margarine

1 baked (9-inch) pie shell

2 cups shredded Swiss or provolone cheese

½ cup vegetable broth

½ cup milk

2 eggs or equivalent amount of egg substitute

3 tablespoons flour

1 tablespoon freshly ground pepper

⅛ teaspoon nutmeg

- ◆ Sauté the onions in the olive oil and margarine in a skillet until golden brown.

- ◆ Arrange the onions in the pie shell. Sprinkle with the cheese.

- ◆ Whisk the broth, milk, eggs, flour, pepper and nutmeg in a bowl until blended. Pour over the prepared layers.

- ◆ Bake at 375 degrees for 30 minutes or until golden brown.

Garlic Mashed Potatoes

Serves 4

3 large Yukon gold potatoes, cut into quarters

6 cloves of garlic, chopped

¼ cup olive oil

salt and freshly ground pepper to taste

1 cup milk or buttermilk

¼ cup butter or margarine, softened

◆ Combine the potatoes with enough water to cover in a saucepan.

◆ Bring to a boil; reduce heat.

◆ Simmer until tender. Drain, reserving a small amount of the cooking liquid.

◆ Mash the potatoes, garlic and reserved cooking liquid in a bowl. Add the olive oil, salt and pepper and beat until blended. Stir in the milk and butter.

◆ Whisk until fluffy.

◆ Taste and adjust the seasonings.

 Spinach Pie   Serves 6

¹/₂ cup butter, chilled, cut into 5 or 6 pieces

1¹/₃ cups flour

¹/₄ cup ice water

1 (10-ounce) package frozen chopped spinach, thawed, drained

1 cup light sour cream

4 eggs

³/₄ teaspoon salt

¹/₂ teaspoon nutmeg

¹/₂ teaspoon pepper

1 cup bread crumbs

1 cup shredded Swiss cheese

3 tablespoons melted butter

- ◆ Combine ¹/₂ cup butter and flour in a food processor container.

- ◆ Process until crumbly.

- ◆ Add the ice water gradually, processing constantly until the mixture forms a ball.

- ◆ Roll into a 12-inch circle on a lightly floured surface. Fit into a 8- or 9-inch pie plate. Flute the edge.

- ◆ Bake at 450 degrees for 12 minutes.

- ◆ Let stand until cool.

- ◆ Squeeze the moisture from the spinach. Spread in the pie shell.

- ◆ Whisk the sour cream, eggs, salt, nutmeg and pepper in a bowl until blended. Pour over the spinach.

- ◆ Combine the bread crumbs, cheese and 3 tablespoons butter in a bowl, tossing to mix. Sprinkle over the top.

- ◆ Bake at 350 degrees for 30 minutes.

Butternut Squash Soufflé

Serves 12 to 15

2 butternut squash

1³/₄ cups sugar

1 (12-ounce) can evaporated
    skim milk

1 cup melted butter or
    margarine

³/₄ cup flour

4 eggs or equivalent amount of
    egg substitute, beaten

1 tablespoon vanilla extract

◆ Cut the squash lengthwise into halves; discard
the seeds.

◆ Place the squash cut side down in a baking pan. Add
water to measure 1 inch.

◆ Bake at 350 degrees for 1 hour; drain.

◆ Let stand until cool.

◆ Scoop the pulp into a food processor container. Add
the sugar, evaporated skim milk, butter, flour, eggs
and vanilla.

◆ Process until blended.

◆ Pour the squash mixture into a 9x13-inch baking
dish or 2-quart soufflé dish sprayed with nonstick
cooking spray.

◆ Bake at 350 degrees for 30 minutes.

Variation:
Substitute 2 packages of frozen carrots for the squash
for a Carrot Soufflé.

Squash Casserole

Serves 12

3 pounds squash, sliced

1 large onion, sliced

2 cups herb dressing mix

2 cups shredded Cheddar cheese

1 (10-ounce) can reduced-calorie cream of chicken soup

1 cup light sour cream

1/2 cup melted butter

2 eggs or equivalent amount of egg substitute, beaten

salt and pepper to taste

shredded Cheddar cheese to taste (optional)

◆ Combine the squash and onion in a steamer.

◆ Steam until tender.

◆ Mash the squash and onion in a bowl and drain.

◆ Combine the dressing mix, 2 cups cheese, soup, sour cream, butter, eggs, salt and pepper in a bowl and mix well. Stir in the squash mixture.

◆ Spoon into a 9x13-inch baking dish sprayed with nonstick cooking spray. Sprinkle with cheese to taste.

◆ Bake at 350 degrees for 50 to 60 minutes or until brown and bubbly.

Variation:
Substitute reduced-calorie cream of mushroom soup for the cream of chicken soup.

Fresh Tomato Tart

Serves 8

1 all ready pie pastry

1 cup shredded mozzarella cheese

1 cup shredded Swiss cheese

1/2 cup chopped fresh basil

3 or 4 large tomatoes, peeled, cut into 1/2-inch slices

2 tablespoons olive oil

1/2 cup chopped fresh basil

1 teaspoon freshly cracked pepper

◆ Fit the pastry into a 10-inch tart pan. Trim the edge and prick the bottom and side of the pastry with a fork.

◆ Bake using package directions.

◆ Sprinkle the bottom of the tart shell with a mixture of the mozzarella cheese and Swiss cheese. Top with 1/2 cup basil.

◆ Arrange the tomato slices in a decorative pattern over the basil. Brush with the olive oil.

◆ Sprinkle with 1/2 cup basil and pepper.

◆ Bake at 400 degrees for 8 to 10 minutes.

 Confit of Vegetables
Serves 12

4 medium onions, sliced

3 tablespoons chopped fresh thyme

4 cloves of garlic, finely chopped

2 tablespoons olive oil

salt and pepper to taste

2 ripe tomatoes, thinly sliced

1 medium zucchini, thinly sliced

1 eggplant, thinly sliced

1/4 cup olive oil

grated Parmesan cheese to taste

◆ Cook the onions, thyme and garlic in 2 tablespoons olive oil in a heavy sauté pan or iron skillet over low heat for 12 minutes or until the onions are tender, stirring frequently. Season with salt and pepper.

◆ Spread the onion mixture evenly in a 9x13-inch baking dish.

◆ Arrange the tomatoes, zucchini and eggplant in overlapping alternating layers over the onions.

◆ Drizzle with 1/4 cup olive oil. Sprinkle with salt and pepper.

◆ Bake at 325 degrees for 30 minutes or until the vegetables are tender. Sprinkle with Parmesan cheese.

◆ Increase the oven temperature to 475 degrees.

◆ Cook for 5 minutes longer or until light brown.

◆ Serve immediately.

Spicy Oriental Stir-Fry

Serves 4 to 6

6 tablespoons sesame seeds

2 tablespoons canola oil

1 teaspoon chile oil

2 medium onions, chopped

1 head of garlic, separated into
cloves, sliced

2 tablespoons chopped
gingerroot

2 medium zucchini, sliced

2 medium yellow squash, sliced

½ yellow bell pepper, sliced

3 tablespoons hoisin sauce

2 tablespoons oyster sauce

2 tablespoons lite soy sauce

1 large tomato, seeded, chopped

1 (8-ounce) can water chestnuts,
drained, sliced

1 (8-ounce) can bamboo shoots,
drained, sliced

◆ Spread the sesame seeds in a single layer on a
nonstick baking sheet.

◆ Toast at 350 degrees for 10 minutes.

◆ Combine the canola oil and chile oil in a large
skillet or wok.

◆ Heat until hot but not smoking. Stir in the onions,
garlic and gingerroot.

◆ Stir-fry just until the garlic begins to turn golden
brown. Add the zucchini, yellow squash and yellow
pepper and mix well.

◆ Stir-fry until the vegetables are tender-crisp.

◆ Stir in the hoisin sauce, oyster sauce and soy sauce.
Add the tomato, water chestnuts and bamboo shoots
and mix well.

◆ Cook until heated through, stirring constantly.

◆ Sprinkle with the sesame seeds.

◆ Serve immediately.

 Goat Cheese and Mushroom Pizza Serves 4

1½ cups thawed frozen spinach

2 tablespoons (or more) olive oil

1 cup chopped shallots

2 cups thinly sliced white mushrooms

1½ cups thinly sliced shiitake mushrooms

3 cloves of garlic, thinly sliced

½ teaspoon sugar

1 Boboli

6 ounces herbed goat cheese, crumbled

◆ Squeeze the moisture from the spinach.

◆ Heat the olive oil in a sauté pan until hot. Stir in the shallots, mushrooms and garlic.

◆ Cook just until golden brown, stirring constantly. Sprinkle with the sugar and mix lightly. Remove from heat.

◆ Place the Boboli on a nonstick baking sheet.

◆ Spread the mushroom mixture over the Boboli.

◆ Top with the spinach. Sprinkle with the goat cheese.

◆ Bake at 425 degrees for 12 to 15 minutes or until bubbly.

◆ Serve hot.

Pasta

 Tricolor Tortellini Salad   *Serves 8*

For the Pesto

1 cup fresh basil

1 cup fresh parsley

1/3 cup mixture of pine nuts and walnuts

1/3 cup grated Parmesan cheese

1/4 cup olive oil

5 cloves of garlic

salt and freshly ground pepper to taste

1/4 cup warm water

For the Salad

1 (16-ounce) package tricolor tortellini, cooked, drained

1 (14-ounce) can artichokes, drained, cut into quarters

1 (14-ounce) can hearts of palm, drained, sliced

1 red bell pepper, roasted, seeded, peeled, julienned

1 yellow bell pepper, roasted, seeded, peeled, julienned

1 bunch asparagus, blanched, cut into 1-inch pieces

1 pint cherry tomatoes

◆ To prepare the pesto, combine the basil, parsley, nuts, cheese, olive oil, garlic, salt and pepper in a food processor container.

◆ Add the warm water in a fine stream, processing constantly until of the desired consistency. Add additional water for a thinner consistency.

◆ Taste and adjust the seasonings.

◆ To prepare the salad, toss the tortellini with the pesto in a bowl.

◆ Add the artichokes, hearts of palm, red pepper, yellow pepper, asparagus and cherry tomatoes and toss gently.

Linguini with Parsley Pesto Sauce

Serves 4

1 (8-ounce) package linguini

1 tablespoon salt

3 quarts boiling water

1 clove of garlic

2 tablespoons pine nuts

3 cups parsley sprigs, stems
removed

3¹/2 tablespoons olive oil

2 tablespoons freshly grated
Parmesan cheese

¹/2 teaspoon dried basil

¹/8 teaspoon salt

¹/8 teaspoon pepper

◆ Combine the linguini and 1 tablespoon salt with the
boiling water in a saucepan.

◆ Cook until al dente; drain. Cover to keep warm.

◆ Combine the garlic and pine nuts in a blender
container.

◆ Process until finely chopped.

◆ Add the parsley and olive oil gradually, processing
constantly until smooth. Stop blender periodically
to push down the parsley with a spatula.

◆ Add the cheese, basil, ¹/8 teaspoon salt and pepper.

◆ Process until blended.

◆ Toss the sauce with the hot linguini in a
serving bowl.

◆ Serve immediately.

 Pasta with Artichoke Hearts   Serves 4

1 (14-ounce) can artichoke
  hearts

½ cup sliced black olives

¼ cup olive oil

3 tablespoons fresh lemon juice

2 cloves of garlic, chopped

¼ teaspoon crumbled dried red
  chile pepper

salt and freshly ground pepper
  to taste

1 (16-ounce) package linguini,
  cooked, drained

sliced Italian pepperoni,
  julienned

◆ Drain the artichokes and pat dry. Cut lengthwise
  into slices.

◆ Combine the artichokes, black olives, olive oil,
  lemon juice, garlic, chile pepper, salt and pepper
  in a bowl and mix gently.

◆ Let stand at room temperature for 1 hour.

◆ Combine the linguini with the artichoke mixture in
  a bowl and toss gently.

◆ Top with pepperoni.

◆ Serve immediately.

Note:
Serve with crusty sliced Italian bread.

Baked Macaroni and Cheese

Serves 4 to 6

1 (8-ounce) package elbow
  macaroni

¹/₂ cup butter or margarine

¹/₂ cup flour

1 teaspoon salt

¹/₄ teaspoon pepper

¹/₄ teaspoon nutmeg

2 cups milk

2 cups shredded Cheddar cheese

- ◆ Cook the macaroni using package directions; drain.
- ◆ Heat the butter in a saucepan until melted. Remove from heat.
- ◆ Add the flour, salt, pepper and nutmeg, stirring until smooth. Stir in the milk gradually.
- ◆ Bring to a boil, stirring constantly; reduce heat.
- ◆ Simmer for 1 minute, stirring constantly. Remove from heat.
- ◆ Stir in 1¹/₂ cups of the cheese. Spoon into a 1¹/₂-quart baking dish. Sprinkle with the remaining ¹/₂ cup cheese.
- ◆ Bake at 375 degrees for 20 to 30 minutes or until golden brown.

Garlic Orzo

Serves 6

8 to 10 cloves of garlic, sliced

1 tablespoon olive oil

¹/₂ cup orzo

¹/₂ cup rice

1 (14-ounce) can chicken or
  vegetable broth

¹/₃ cup sliced green onions

¹/₃ cup thinly sliced fresh basil
  leaves

¹/₄ cup chopped fresh parsley

- ◆ Sauté the garlic in the olive oil in a skillet just until golden brown. Stir in the orzo and rice.
- ◆ Sauté until the pasta and rice are light brown. Add the broth gradually, stirring constantly.
- ◆ Simmer, covered, for 20 minutes or until the broth has been absorbed. Remove from heat.
- ◆ Add the green onions, basil and parsley and toss lightly.

Pasta with Wild Mushroom Sauce   Serves 4 to 6

1/4 cup olive oil

2 cups chopped purple onions

6 large cloves of garlic, chopped

1 1/2 pounds mixed fresh wild mushrooms (portobello, oyster, shiitake)

3 tablespoons unsalted butter

2 tablespoons chopped fresh thyme

1 teaspoon freshly cracked pepper

1 3/4 cups canned vegetable broth

8 ounces feta cheese, crumbled

1/2 cup chopped fresh parsley

1/2 cup julienned fresh basil

hot cooked pasta

grated Parmesan cheese

- ◆ Heat the olive oil in a large skillet over medium-high heat until hot. Add the onions and garlic.

- ◆ Sauté until brown. Stir in the mushrooms.

- ◆ Cook just until the mushrooms begin to release liquid. Remove from heat.

- ◆ Add the butter, thyme and pepper and mix well.

- ◆ Cook for 2 minutes, stirring constantly.

- ◆ Add the broth and mix well. Bring to a light boil.

- ◆ Boil for 5 minutes or until thickened, stirring constantly. Remove from heat.

- ◆ Stir in the feta cheese, parsley and basil.

- ◆ Spoon over cooked pasta of your choice on a serving platter. Sprinkle generously with Parmesan cheese.

Shrimp with Feta Cheese Sauce

Serves 4

1 pound large shrimp, cooked

1 pound feta cheese, drained, crumbled

4 large tomatoes, peeled, seeded, coarsely chopped

6 green onions, sliced

4 teaspoons minced fresh oregano

2 teaspoons minced fresh thyme

Juice of 1 lemon

salt and freshly ground pepper to taste

1 (16-ounce) package pasta, cooked, drained

- ◆ Peel the shrimp, leaving the tails in tact.
- ◆ Combine the shrimp, feta cheese, tomatoes, green onions, oregano, thyme, lemon juice, salt and pepper in a bowl and toss gently.
- ◆ Let stand at room temperature for 1 hour.
- ◆ Arrange the pasta on a large serving platter. Spoon the shrimp mixture over the pasta.
- ◆ Serve immediately.

Note:
May substitute 1 1/2 teaspoons dried crumbled oregano for the fresh oregano and 2 teaspoons dried crumbled thyme for the fresh thyme.

# Penne with Basil Tomato Sauce

Serves 4

1 (16-ounce) package penne

¼ cup (or less) olive oil

¼ cup pine nuts

4 cloves of garlic, sliced

6 large tomatoes, peeled, seeded, chopped

2 cups chopped fresh basil

1 teaspoon freshly cracked pepper

⅓ cup grated Parmesan cheese

- ◆ Cook the pasta using package directions; drain.
- ◆ Heat the olive oil in a skillet until hot. Add the pine nuts and garlic.
- ◆ Sauté until the garlic is golden brown. Stir in the tomatoes.
- ◆ Simmer until the tomatoes begin to breakup, stirring frequently. The sauce should be chunky. Stir in the basil.
- ◆ Cook for 3 minutes, stirring frequently. Add the pepper and mix well. Remove from heat.
- ◆ Sprinkle with the cheese and stir lightly.
- ◆ Spoon over the pasta on a serving platter.
- ◆ Sprinkle with additional Parmesan cheese if desired.

Penne with Tomatoes and Vodka

Serves 4

2 tablespoons butter

1 medium onion, chopped

2 cloves of garlic, chopped

1 tablespoon dried Italian
   seasoning, crumbled

1 pound fresh Italian plum
   tomatoes, chopped

3 ounces sliced prosciutto,
   chopped

1/2 cup vodka

3/4 cup whipping cream

1/2 cup grated Parmesan cheese

1 (8-ounce) package penne,
   cooked, drained

1/4 cup thinly sliced fresh basil
   leaves

salt and pepper to taste

1/2 cup grated Parmesan cheese

◆ Heat the butter in a skillet over medium-high heat until melted. Stir in the onion, garlic and Italian seasoning.

◆ Sauté for 6 minutes or until the onion is tender. Add the tomatoes and prosciutto and mix well.

◆ Simmer for 10 minutes, stirring occasionally. Stir in the vodka.

◆ Simmer for 5 minutes, stirring occasionally. Add the whipping cream and 1/2 cup cheese and mix well.

◆ Simmer for 4 minutes or until slightly thickened, stirring frequently. Add the pasta and basil, tossing to coat.

◆ Season with salt and pepper.

◆ Serve with 1/2 cup Parmesan cheese.

# Vermicelli with Broccoli Pesto Sauce   Serves 4

1 (12-ounce) package vermicelli

salt to taste

4 cups fresh broccoli florets

1/4 cup pine nuts

2 cloves of garlic

3 1/2 tablespoons olive oil

6 tablespoons freshly grated
  Parmesan cheese

2 tablespoons thinly sliced fresh
  basil leaves

freshly cracked pepper to taste

- ◆ Add the vermicelli and salt gradually to boiling water in a saucepan so that the water continues to boil.

- ◆ Boil until tender, stirring occasionally. Drain in a colander. Cover to keep warm.

- ◆ Cook the broccoli in boiling salted water in a saucepan for 5 to 6 minutes or until the stalk portion is tender. Plunge into cold water.

- ◆ Let stand until cool; drain.

- ◆ Combine the pine nuts and garlic in a blender container.

- ◆ Process until finely chopped.

- ◆ Add the broccoli, olive oil, cheese, basil and pepper in several batches, processing constantly just until the mixture is almost smooth and scraping the side of the blender occasionally. The sauce should have a slightly coarse texture.

- ◆ Toss the sauce with the hot cooked vermicelli in a bowl.

White Beans and Spinach with Pasta   Serves 6

2 cups small, shaped pasta
   (wheels, radiatore, shells)

2 tablespoons olive oil

1½ cups sliced onions

4 cloves of garlic, sliced

½ cup vegetable broth

8 cups fresh spinach

4 red and yellow tomatoes,
   seeded, coarsely chopped

1 (15-ounce) can cannellini
   beans, drained

1 cup grated Parmesan cheese

salt and pepper to taste

- ◆ Cook the pasta using package directions; drain.

- ◆ Heat the olive oil in a heavy skillet until hot. Add the onions and garlic.

- ◆ Sauté until golden brown. Stir in the broth.

- ◆ Arrange the spinach over the top.

- ◆ Cook for 3 minutes. Add the tomatoes and mix well.

- ◆ Cook for 3 minutes, stirring occasionally. Remove from heat.

- ◆ Combine the pasta, beans and cheese in a bowl, tossing to mix. Add the spinach mixture and mix gently.

- ◆ Season with salt and pepper.

Note:
May substitute white navy beans for the cannellini beans.

 # Noodle Kugel

Serves 6

1 (12-ounce) package wide egg
   noodles
2 eggs
³/₄ cup sugar
¹/₂ cup melted butter, cooled
2 tablespoons cinnamon
1 teaspoon salt

- ◆ Cook the noodles using package directions; drain.

- ◆ Beat the eggs in a bowl until blended.

- ◆ Stir in the sugar, butter, cinnamon and salt. Add the noodles and mix well.

- ◆ Spoon into a round baking dish sprayed with nonstick cooking spray.

- ◆ Bake, covered with a glass top, at 350 degrees for 2 hours. The top and bottom will be brown.

Breads

 # Cheese Biscuits

Makes 24 biscuits

1 cup shredded sharp Cheddar
  cheese
1 cup flour
1 cup crisp rice cereal
1/2 cup butter, softened
1/8 teaspoon cayenne

- ◆ Combine the cheese, flour, cereal, butter and cayenne in a bowl and mix well.
- ◆ Shape by teaspoonfuls into balls.
- ◆ Place the dough balls on an ungreased baking sheet.
- ◆ Chill for 10 minutes.
- ◆ Bake at 400 degrees for 10 to 12 minutes or just until light brown.

 # Sour Cream Biscuits

Makes 24 biscuits

1/2 cup melted butter
1 cup sour cream
2 cups baking mix

- ◆ Combine the butter and sour cream in a bowl and mix well.
- ◆ Add the baking mix, stirring until blended.
- ◆ Spoon the dough into miniature muffin cups.
- ◆ Bake at 375 degrees for 15 minutes.

Onion Corn Bread

Serves 8

¹/₄ cup butter or margarine

1¹/₂ cups chopped onions

1 cup sour cream

¹/₂ cup shredded sharp Cheddar
cheese

¹/₄ teaspoon salt

1 (10- to 12-ounce) package corn
muffin mix

1 (9-ounce) can cream-style corn

¹/₂ cup skim milk

1 egg, beaten

2 to 4 drops of red pepper sauce

¹/₂ cup shredded sharp Cheddar
cheese

◆ Heat the butter in a skillet over medium heat until
melted. Add the onions.

◆ Sauté for 10 minutes or until tender. Cool slightly.

◆ Stir in the sour cream, ¹/₂ cup cheese and salt.

◆ Combine the corn muffin mix, corn, skim milk, egg
and red pepper sauce in a bowl and mix well.

◆ Spoon the batter into a greased 8x8-inch baking pan.
Spread the onion mixture evenly over the batter.
Sprinkle with ¹/₂ cup cheese.

◆ Bake at 425 degrees for 30 to 35 minutes or until a
wooden pick inserted in the center comes out clean.

◆ Serve warm.

 Savory Dill Bread

Makes 1 loaf

1 envelope dry yeast
1/4 cup lukewarm water
1 cup low-fat cottage cheese
2 tablespoons sugar
2 tablespoons minced onion
1 tablespoon butter
2 teaspoons dillseeds
1 teaspoon salt
2 1/4 to 2 1/2 cups flour
1/4 teaspoon baking soda
melted butter (optional)
salt to taste (optional)

- ◆ Dissolve the yeast in the lukewarm water and mix well.

- ◆ Heat the cottage cheese in a saucepan until lukewarm. Stir in the yeast, sugar, onion, 1 tablespoon butter, dillseeds and 1 teaspoon salt.

- ◆ Combine the flour and baking soda in a bowl and mix well. Add to the cottage cheese mixture and mix well.

- ◆ Let rise for 1 hour. Punch the dough down.

- ◆ Shape into a loaf in a greased loaf pan.

- ◆ Let rise for 30 to 40 minutes.

- ◆ Bake at 350 degrees for 40 to 50 minutes or until the loaf tests done.

- ◆ Brush the top with melted butter to taste and sprinkle with salt to taste.

 Blueberry Sally Lunn Bead

Serves 8

2 cups sifted flour

1 tablespoon baking powder

1/2 teaspoon salt

1/2 cup butter or margarine, softened

1/2 cup sugar

2 eggs or equivalent amount of egg substitute

3/4 cup evaporated skim milk

1 cup fresh blueberries

1/4 cup packed light brown sugar

1 teaspoon cinnamon

- ◆ Mix the flour, baking powder and salt together.
- ◆ Combine the butter, sugar and eggs in a mixer bowl.
- ◆ Beat at low speed just until combined.
- ◆ Beat at high speed until light and fluffy, scraping the bowl occasionally.
- ◆ Add the dry ingredients alternately with the evaporated skim milk, mixing well after each addition.
- ◆ Fold in the blueberries.
- ◆ Spoon into a greased 8x8-inch baking pan. Sprinkle with the brown sugar and cinnamon.
- ◆ Bake at 375 degrees for 35 minutes.
- ◆ Serve warm.

Note:
May substitute 3 ounces Chukar blueberries or cherries for the fresh blueberries.

 Zucchini Bread

Makes 2 to 3 loaves

For the Bread

3 cups unbleached flour

1½ cups sugar

1 tablespoon cinnamon

1 teaspoon salt

1 teaspoon baking soda

1 teaspoon baking powder

3 cups shredded zucchini

1½ cups dark raisins

1½ cups golden raisins

1 cup chopped walnuts

1 cup extra-virgin olive oil

3 eggs

2 teaspoons vanilla extract

For the Lemon Icing

1½ cups confectioners' sugar, sifted

3 tablespoons fresh lemon juice

1 tablespoon butter, softened

1 teaspoon grated lemon zest

◆ To prepare the bread, sift the flour into a bowl. Add the sugar, cinnamon, salt, baking soda, baking powder, zucchini, raisins, and walnuts, whisking well after each addition.

◆ Whisk the olive oil, eggs and vanilla in a bowl until blended. Add to the flour mixture and mix well.

◆ Spoon into 2 or 3 loaf pans sprayed with nonstick cooking spray.

◆ Bake at 350 degrees for 1 hour and 20 minutes.

◆ Cool slightly in pans. Invert onto a wire rack to cool completely.

◆ For the icing, combine the confectioners' sugar, lemon juice, butter and lemon zest in a mixer bowl.

◆ Beat until blended, scraping the bowl occasionally.

◆ Spread over the tops of the cooled bread loaves.

# Butter Batter Bread

Makes 3 loaves

4 envelopes dry yeast
2 cups lukewarm water
2 cups milk
5 tablespoons butter
1/4 cup honey
2 tablespoons salt
8 1/2 cups unbleached flour
melted butter

- ◆ Dissolve the yeast in the lukewarm water in a bowl and mix well.

- ◆ Combine the milk, 5 tablespoons butter, honey and salt in a saucepan.

- ◆ Heat just until blended, stirring frequently. Add to the yeast mixture and mix well. Stir in the flour.

- ◆ Let rise, covered, until doubled in bulk. Punch the dough down.

- ◆ Beat for 30 seconds.

- ◆ Shape into loaves in 3 greased loaf pans.

- ◆ Let rise for 10 minutes.

- ◆ Bake at 375 degrees for 50 minutes. Brush the tops with melted butter.

- ◆ Bake for 10 minutes longer.

 Friday Night Challah

Makes 1 loaf

1 cup lukewarm water
1 envelope dry yeast
2½ tablespoons sugar
2 tablespoons honey
2 teaspoons salt
¼ cup vegetable oil
2 eggs, beaten
3½ cups bread flour
1 egg yolk, beaten
sesame or poppy seeds
  (optional)

- ◆ Pour the lukewarm water into a mixer bowl. Sprinkle with the yeast and stir until dissolved.

- ◆ Stir in the sugar, honey, salt and mix well. Beat in the oil and eggs.

- ◆ Add 3 cups of the bread flour gradually, beating well after each addition.

- ◆ Knead on a lightly floured surface for 4 minutes or until smooth and elastic, adding the remaining ½ cup flour as needed.

- ◆ Place the dough in a lightly oiled bowl, turning to coat the surface.

- ◆ Let rise, covered with a warm damp towel, in a draft-free place for 2 to 3 hours or until triple in size.

- ◆ Turn the dough onto a lightly floured surface and punch down.

- ◆ Divide the dough into 3 equal portions. Roll each portion into a rope 1½ inches thick.

- ◆ Twist into a braid on a nonstick baking sheet. Brush with the egg yolk. Sprinkle with sesame or poppy seeds.

- ◆ Let rise for 15 minutes.

- ◆ Bake at 350 degrees for 1 hour.

 Filled Coffee Ring

Serves 12

For the Coffee Ring

2 envelopes dry yeast

$\frac{1}{2}$ cup warm (105 to 115 degree) water

$1\frac{1}{2}$ cups lukewarm milk

$\frac{1}{2}$ cup sugar

2 teaspoons salt

$\frac{1}{2}$ cup vegetable oil

2 eggs, beaten

$6\frac{1}{2}$ to $7\frac{1}{2}$ cups flour

$\frac{1}{4}$ cup melted butter or margarine

$\frac{1}{2}$ cup sugar

$\frac{1}{4}$ cup cinnamon

$\frac{1}{2}$ cup golden raisins

$\frac{1}{2}$ cup chopped pecans

$\frac{1}{4}$ cup chopped maraschino cherries

For the Creamy Frosting

1 cup whipping cream

1 cup sugar

1 teaspoon vanilla extract

◆ For the ring, dissolve the yeast in the warm water and mix well. Let stand for 5 minutes.

◆ Combine the milk, $\frac{1}{2}$ cup sugar and salt in a bowl and mix well. Stir in the yeast mixture, oil and eggs.

◆ Add the flour gradually, stirring until a soft but slightly sticky dough forms and mix well.

◆ Let rise, covered, in a warm draft-free place for 1 hour or until doubled in bulk.

◆ Knead on a lightly floured surface for 5 minutes or until smooth and elastic. Place the dough in a bowl.

◆ Let rise, covered, for 40 minutes or until doubled in bulk.

◆ Roll into a 12x21-inch rectangle on a lightly floured surface. Brush with the melted butter. Sprinkle with $\frac{1}{2}$ cup sugar, cinnamon, raisins, pecans and cherries. Roll as for a jelly roll and pinch edge to seal.

◆ Shape into a ring on a greased baking sheet and pinch the ends to seal.

◆ Cut $\frac{2}{3}$ through the ring from the outside edge at 1-inch intervals with kitchen shears or a sharp knife.

◆ Let rise, covered, in a warm draft-free place for 30 minutes or until doubled in bulk.

◆ Bake at 350 degrees for 20 to 25 minutes or until the ring tests done.

◆ For the frosting, combine the whipping cream, sugar and vanilla in a saucepan and mix well.

◆ Cook over low heat to 230 degrees on a candy thermometer, soft-ball stage, stirring constantly. Be careful, this mixture has a tendency to boil over if the heat is too high. Remove from heat.

◆ Beat until thickened. Drizzle over the hot ring.

 French Bread   Makes 2 loaves

1 envelope dry yeast or 1 cake yeast
1 cup lukewarm water
1 tablespoon sugar
1 teaspoon salt
2¹/₂ cups bread flour or high gluten flour

- ◆ Combine the yeast and lukewarm water in a bowl, stirring until the yeast dissolves. Stir in the sugar and salt.
- ◆ Add the bread flour gradually, stirring well after each addition.
- ◆ Knead the dough on a lightly floured surface for 5 to 10 minutes or until smooth and elastic.
- ◆ Place the dough in a greased bowl, turning to coat the surface.
- ◆ Let rise, covered with a damp towel, in a draft-free place for 2 to 3 hours or until doubled in bulk. Punch the dough down.
- ◆ Divide into 2 equal portions.
- ◆ Roll each portion into a long slender loaf. Place each loaf into an oiled French bread loaf pan.
- ◆ Let rise for 30 minutes.
- ◆ Bake at 425 degrees for 40 minutes.

Onion Poppy Seed Bread

Makes 1 loaf

For the Filling
1 cup finely chopped onion

1/4 cup melted butter or
    margarine

1/4 cup poppy seeds

1/4 teaspoon salt

For the Bread
1 envelope dry yeast

1/4 cup lukewarm water

4 1/2 to 5 cups flour

1 cup milk, heated

1/2 cup melted butter or
    margarine

1/4 cup sugar

1 1/2 teaspoons salt

1 egg, beaten

1 egg, beaten

chopped onion (optional)

poppy seeds (optional)

- To prepare the filling, combine the onion, butter, poppy seeds and salt in a bowl and mix well.

- To prepare the bread, dissolve the yeast in the lukewarm water in a mixer bowl and mix well. Stir in 2 cups of the flour.

- Add the milk, butter, sugar, salt and 1 egg and mix well. Beat at medium speed for 2 minutes, scraping the bowl occasionally.

- Stir in enough of the remaining flour (about 2 cups) with a wooden spoon to make a stiff dough.

- Knead on a lightly floured surface for 8 to 10 minutes or until smooth and elastic. Place the dough in a greased bowl, turning to coat the surface.

- Let rise, covered, in a warm draft-free place for 1 hour or until doubled in bulk. Punch the dough down.

- Roll into an 8x20-inch rectangle on a lightly floured surface. Cut the rectangle into halves to form two 4x20-inch rectangles.

- Spread the filling over the rectangles to within 1/2 inch of the edges.

- Fold the long edges of 1 of the rectangles together. Pinch the edge to seal forming a long rope.

- Repeat the process with the remaining rectangle.

- Twist the ropes together. Shape into a ring on a lightly greased baking sheet.

- Let rise, covered, in a warm draft-free place for 1 hour or until doubled in bulk.

- Brush with 1 egg. Sprinkle with additional chopped onion and poppy seeds.

- Bake at 350 degrees for 40 minutes or until the ring sounds hollow when tapped. Remove to a wire rack to cool slightly.

Buttermilk Pan Rolls

Makes 36 rolls

2 envelopes dry yeast
1/2 cup lukewarm water
6 cups flour
2 teaspoons salt
1 teaspoon baking soda
1 cup buttermilk
1 cup vegetable shortening
3/4 cup sugar
1/2 cup water
1 egg, beaten
melted butter

- ◆ Dissolve the yeast in 1/2 cup lukewarm water and mix well.
- ◆ Sift the flour and salt into a bowl and mix well.
- ◆ Dissolve the baking soda in the buttermilk and mix well.
- ◆ Heat the shortening in a saucepan until melted. Stir in the sugar and 1/2 cup water.
- ◆ Let stand until cool.
- ◆ Add the buttermilk mixture and egg to the shortening mixture and mix well. Stir in the yeast mixture.
- ◆ Add to the dry ingredients gradually, stirring until mixed. Chill for 1 hour.
- ◆ Roll into a circle on a lightly floured surface. Cut with a round cutter or the bottom of a glass.
- ◆ Fold each dough circle into halves and place with sides touching on a baking sheet. Brush with melted butter.
- ◆ Let rise in a warm place for 1 1/2 hours.
- ◆ Bake at 400 to 425 degrees for 10 minutes or until golden brown.

Cakes

Applesauce Date Cake

Serves 16

2 cups flour

2 teaspoons baking soda

1 teaspoon cinnamon

1/2 teaspoon allspice

1/2 teaspoon nutmeg

1/4 teaspoon ground cloves

1/4 teaspoon salt

2 eggs

1 cup packed light brown sugar

1/2 cup butter or margarine,
  softened

2 cups applesauce, heated

1 cup chopped dates

3/4 cup coarsely chopped walnuts

Cream Cheese Frosting
  (page 141)

◆ Sift the flour, baking soda, cinnamon, allspice, nutmeg, cloves and salt into a mixer bowl and stir to mix.

◆ Add the eggs, brown sugar, butter and 1 cup of the applesauce, beating at low speed after each addition.

◆ Beat at medium speed for 2 minutes, scraping the bowl occasionally. Add the remaining 1 cup applesauce, dates and walnuts.

◆ Beat for 1 minute.

◆ Spoon into a greased and floured 8x8-inch cake pan.

◆ Bake at 350 degrees for 50 minutes or until a wooden pick inserted in the center of the cake comes out clean.

◆ Cool in pan on a wire rack for 10 minutes. Invert onto wire rack to cool completely.

◆ Spread the Cream Cheese Frosting over the top of the cake.

 Chocolate Cake   Serves 12

1½ cups cake flour

1¼ cups sugar

½ cup baking cocoa

1 teaspoon baking soda

¾ teaspoon salt

¼ teaspoon cream of tartar

1 cup milk

⅔ cup vegetable shortening

2 eggs

1 teaspoon vanilla extract

◆ Grease and flour the bottoms of 2 cake pans.

◆ Sift the cake flour, sugar, baking cocoa, baking soda, salt and cream of tartar into a mixer bowl and stir to mix.

◆ Add ⅔ cup of the milk and shortening.

◆ Beat at low speed for 2 minutes, scraping the bowl occasionally.

◆ Add the eggs 1 at a time, beating well after each addition.

◆ Add the remaining ⅓ cup milk and vanilla.

◆ Beat for 2 minutes, scraping the bowl occasionally. Spoon into the prepared cake pans.

◆ Bake at 350 degrees for 30 to 45 minutes or until the layers test done.

◆ Cool in pans on a wire rack for 10 minutes. Invert onto wire rack to cool completely.

◆ Spread your favorite frosting between the layers and over the top and side of the cake.

 Joannie's Chocolate Cake   Serves 12

For the Cake

2 cups cake flour

1 teaspoon baking soda

1 cup buttermilk

2 ounces bittersweet chocolate, melted

1¼ cups sugar

½ cup butter, softened

2 eggs

1 teaspoon vanilla extract

For the Chocolate Frosting

1½ cups milk

1½ cups sugar

1 tablespoon butter

3 ounces unsweetened chocolate

3 tablespoons (heaping) cornstarch

1½ teaspoons vanilla extract

- ◆ To prepare the cake, sift the cake flour twice.
- ◆ Dissolve the baking soda in the buttermilk and mix well.
- ◆ Beat the chocolate, sugar and butter in a mixer bowl until creamy, scraping the bowl occasionally. Add the eggs.
- ◆ Beat until blended.
- ◆ Add the cake flour and buttermilk mixture alternately, mixing well after each addition. Beat in the vanilla.
- ◆ Spoon into 2 greased 9-inch-round cake pans.
- ◆ Bake at 350 degrees for 20 minutes.
- ◆ Cool in pans on a wire rack for 10 minutes. Invert onto wire rack to cool completely.
- ◆ To prepare the frosting, combine the milk, sugar, butter, chocolate and cornstarch in a saucepan.
- ◆ Cook until thick and creamy, stirring constantly. Remove from heat. Stir in the vanilla.
- ◆ Beat until the frosting is glossy and of spreading consistency.
- ◆ Let stand until cool.
- ◆ Spread the frosting between the layers and over the top and side of the cake.

Sour Cream Chocolate Cake

Serves 12

flour

1 teaspoon baking soda

1 cup boiling water

2 cups sugar

$1/2$ cup butter, softened

2 eggs

6 tablespoons baking cocoa

1 teaspoon orange juice

$2^1/2$ cups sifted flour

$1/4$ teaspoon salt

1 cup sour cream

- ◆ Spray two 9-inch cake pans with nonstick cooking spray. Dust lightly with flour.

- ◆ Dissolve the baking soda in the boiling water and mix well.

- ◆ Beat the sugar and butter in a mixer bowl until creamy and pale yellow.

- ◆ Add the eggs 1 at a time, beating well after each addition.

- ◆ Beat in the baking cocoa. Mix in the orange juice.

- ◆ Add a mixture of the sifted flour and salt alternately with the sour cream, beginning and ending with the flour mixture and mixing well after each addition.

- ◆ Add the baking soda mixture and mix well. The batter will have a liquid consistency.

- ◆ Pour into the prepared cake pans.

- ◆ Bake at 350 degrees for 35 minutes or until a wooden pick inserted in the center comes out clean.

- ◆ Cool in pans on a wire rack for 10 minutes. Invert onto wire rack to cool completely.

- ◆ Spread with your favorite frosting.

# White Chocolate Butter Cake

Serves 12

1½ cups butter

¾ cup water

4 ounces white chocolate,
   broken into pieces

1½ cups buttermilk

4 eggs, lightly beaten

1½ teaspoons vanilla extract

3½ cups flour

1 cup chopped pecans, toasted

2¼ cups sugar

1½ teaspoons baking soda

Cream Cheese Frosting
   (page 141)

◆ Combine the butter and water in a saucepan.

◆ Bring to a boil over medium heat, stirring until the butter melts. Remove from heat.

◆ Add the white chocolate, stirring until melted. Cool slightly.

◆ Stir in the buttermilk, eggs and vanilla.

◆ Combine ½ cup of the flour and pecans in a bowl, tossing to coat.

◆ Combine the remaining 3 cups flour, sugar and baking soda in a bowl and mix well. Add the white chocolate mixture gradually and mix well. Fold in the pecans. The batter will be light.

◆ Spoon into 3 greased and floured 9-inch-round cake pans.

◆ Bake at 350 degrees for 20 to 25 minutes or until a wooden pick inserted in the center comes out clean.

◆ Cool in pans on wire racks for 10 minutes. Invert onto wire racks to cool completely.

◆ Spread the Cream Cheese Frosting between the layers and over the top and side of the cake.

 Coconut Carrot Cake   Serves 15

For the Cake

2 cups flour

2¹/₂ teaspoons baking soda

2 teaspoons cinnamon

1 teaspoon salt

2 cups sugar

1 cup vegetable oil

3 eggs

2 cups grated carrots

1¹/₂ cups shredded coconut

1 (8-ounce) can juice-pack
  crushed pineapple

¹/₂ cup chopped nuts

**For the Coconut Cream
Frosting**

3 ounces cream cheese, softened

¹/₄ cup butter, softened

3 cups sifted confectioners'
  sugar

1 tablespoon milk

¹/₂ teaspoon vanilla extract

1 cup shredded coconut, toasted

◆ To prepare the cake, mix the flour, baking soda,
  cinnamon and salt in a bowl.

◆ Beat the sugar, oil and eggs in a mixer bowl until
  blended. Add the flour mixture.

◆ Beat until smooth, scraping the bowl occasionally.

◆ Fold in the carrots, coconut, pineapple and nuts.

◆ Spoon into a greased 9x13-inch cake pan.

◆ Bake at 350 degrees for 50 to 60 minutes or until the
  cake tests done.

◆ Cool in pan on a wire rack for 10 minutes. Invert
  onto wire rack to cool completely.

◆ To prepare the frosting, beat the cream cheese and
  butter in a mixer bowl until creamy, scraping the
  bowl occasionally.

◆ Add the confectioners' sugar, milk and vanilla
  alternately, beating well after each addition.

◆ Stir in ¹/₂ cup of the coconut.

◆ Spread the frosting over the top and sides of
  the cake. Sprinkle the top with the remaining
  ¹/₂ cup coconut.

# Traditional Honey Cake   Serves 15

4 cups sifted flour

1 tablespoon baking cocoa

2 teaspoons baking powder

1¹/₂ teaspoons baking soda

¹/₂ teaspoon ground cloves

¹/₂ teaspoon allspice

¹/₂ teaspoon ginger

¹/₂ teaspoon cinnamon

¹/₂ cup chopped walnuts

¹/₂ cup seedless raisins

1¹/₂ cups sugar

5 eggs

¹/₂ cup vegetable oil

1 (16-ounce) jar honey

1 cup strong coffee

◆ Combine the flour, baking cocoa, baking powder, baking soda, cloves, allspice, ginger and cinnamon in a bowl and mix well.

◆ Add the walnuts and raisins and mix well.

◆ Beat the sugar and eggs in a mixer bowl until light and fluffy, scraping the bowl occasionally. Mix in the oil.

◆ Combine the honey and coffee in a bowl and mix well. Add to the egg mixture, beating until blended. Add the flour mixture.

◆ Beat until mixed, scraping the bowl occasionally.

◆ Spoon in a 9x13-inch cake pan.

◆ Bake at 350 degrees for 1 hour.

◆ Cool on a wire rack.

Italian Cream Cake

Serves 15

For the Cake

1 teaspoon baking soda

1 cup buttermilk

2 cups sugar

1/2 cup butter, softened

1/2 cup vegetable oil

5 egg yolks

2 cups flour, sifted

1 cup shredded coconut

1/2 cup chopped nuts

1 teaspoon vanilla extract

5 egg whites

For the Cream Cheese Frosting

8 ounces cream cheese, softened

1/2 cup butter, softened

1 (1-pound) package
   confectioners' sugar

1 teaspoon vanilla extract

1/2 cup finely chopped nuts

- To prepare the cake, dissolve the baking soda in the buttermilk and mix well.

- Beat the sugar, butter and oil in a mixer bowl until creamy, scraping the bowl occasionally.

- Add the egg yolks 1 at a time, beating well after each addition.

- Add the flour and buttermilk mixture alternately, mixing well after each addition.

- Stir in the coconut, nuts and vanilla.

- Beat the egg whites in a mixer bowl until stiff peaks form. Fold into the batter.

- Spoon the batter into a greased and floured 9x13-inch cake pan.

- Bake at 325 degrees for 45 minutes or until the cake tests done.

- Cool in pan on a wire rack.

- To prepare the frosting, beat the cream cheese and butter in a mixer bowl until creamy. Add the confectioners' sugar and vanilla.

- Beat until of spreading consistency, scraping the bowl occasionally. Stir in the nuts.

- Spread over the top of the cake.

Note:
May bake the cake in 3 greased and floured 8- or 9-inch cake pans.

 Caramel-Filled Butter Cake   Serves 12

For the Cake

3 cups sifted cake flour

2¹/₂ teaspoons baking powder

¹/₂ teaspoon salt

1 cup vegetable shortening

2 cups sugar

4 eggs

1 cup milk

1 teaspoon almond extract

1 teaspoon vanilla extract

For the Caramel Filling

3 cups sugar

³/₄ cup milk

1 egg, beaten

¹/₈ teaspoon salt

¹/₂ cup butter, cut up

For the Buttercream Frosting

¹/₃ cup butter or margarine,
   softened

3 cups sifted confectioners'
   sugar

2 to 3 tablespoons half-and-half

¹/₂ teaspoon vanilla extract

1 cup chopped pecans

pecan halves

◆ To prepare the cake, grease three 9-inch cake pans. Line the bottoms with waxed paper and grease Mix cake flour, baking powder and salt in a bowl.

◆ Cream the shortening in a mixer bowl. Add the sugar gradually, beating at medium speed until blended. Add the eggs 1 at a time, beating well after each addition. Add the dry ingredients alternately with the milk, beginning and ending with the dry ingredients. Stir in the flavorings. Spoon evenly into the prepared cake pans.

◆ Bake at 375 degrees for 25 minutes or until layers test done. Cool in pans for 10 minutes. Invert onto wire racks to cool completely.

◆ To prepare the filling, sprinkle ¹/₂ cup of the sugar in a heavy saucepan. Cook over medium heat until the sugar melts and turns a light golden brown in color, stirring constantly. Remove from heat.

◆ Mix the remaining 2¹/₂ cups sugar, milk, egg and salt in a bowl. Stir in the butter. Stir into the hot caramelized sugar. The mixture will tend to lump, but will become smooth with further cooking. Cook over medium heat to 230 degrees on a candy thermometer. Cool for 5 minutes. Beat with a wooden spoon until almost of spreading consistency.

◆ To prepare the frosting, cream the butter in a mixer bowl at medium speed. Add the confectioners' sugar alternately with the half-and-half. Beat until light and fluffy. Stir in the vanilla.

◆ To assemble, spread the filling between the layers and over the top of the cake. Spread the frosting over the side of the cake. Press the chopped pecans into side and place the pecan halves in a decorative pattern on the top of the cake.

Orange Pecan Cake

Serves 12

For the Cake

3¹/₃ cups sifted cake flour

2 teaspoons baking soda

1 teaspoon salt

1¹/₂ cups sugar

¹/₂ cup butter or margarine, softened

¹/₂ cup vegetable shortening

4 eggs

1¹/₂ cups buttermilk

2 cups finely chopped pecans

2 tablespoons grated orange peel

For the Buttercream Frosting

³/₄ cup butter or margarine, softened

¹/₂ cup sifted confectioners' sugar

2 teaspoons vanilla extract

5¹/₂ cups sifted confectioners' sugar

5 to 6 tablespoons milk, cream or evaporated skim milk

pecan halves

◆ To prepare the cake, sift the cake flour, baking soda and salt together.

◆ Beat the sugar, butter and shortening in a mixer bowl until creamy, scraping the bowl occasionally.

◆ Add the eggs 1 at a time, beating well after each addition.

◆ Add the dry ingredients alternately with the buttermilk, beginning and ending with the dry ingredients and mixing well after each addition.

◆ Stir in the pecans and orange peel.

◆ Spoon into 3 greased and floured 9-inch-round cake pans.

◆ Bake at 350 degrees for 25 to 30 minutes or until the layers spring back when touched lightly.

◆ Cool in pans on wire racks for 5 minutes. Invert onto wire racks to cool completely.

◆ For the frosting, beat the butter, ¹/₂ cup confectioners' sugar and vanilla in a mixer bowl until blended.

◆ Beat in the remaining 5¹/₂ cups confectioners' sugar alternately with just enough milk to make of spreading consistency.

◆ Spread the frosting between the layers and over the top and side of the cake. Top with pecan halves.

 Orange Sponge Cake

Serves 16

For the Cake

6 egg yolks

1/2 cup cold water

1 1/2 cups sugar

1/4 teaspoon salt

1 1/2 cups flour

1 teaspoon vanilla extract

6 egg whites

3/4 teaspoon cream of tartar

For the Topping

3/4 cup sugar

2 egg whites

1 cup orange juice

Grated peel of 2 oranges

- ◆ To prepare the cake, beat the egg yolks in a mixer bowl until pale yellow. Add the cold water.

- ◆ Beat until thick.

- ◆ Add the sugar, salt, flour and vanilla in the order listed, mixing well after each addition.

- ◆ Beat the egg whites and cream of tartar in a mixer bowl until stiff peaks form. Fold into the batter.

- ◆ Spoon into an ungreased 10-inch tube pan.

- ◆ Bake at 325 degrees for 1 hour or until the cake tests done and the top is golden brown.

- ◆ Cool in pan on a wire rack.

- ◆ To prepare the topping, beat the sugar and egg whites in a mixer bowl until light and glossy.

- ◆ Add the orange juice and orange peel and mix well.

- ◆ Drizzle over the cake, allowing the topping to flow down the side.

- ◆ Chill, covered, for 12 hours.

Note:
Serve with whipped cream for a real treat.

 Poppy Seed Cake

Serves 16

1½ cups cake flour

1½ teaspoons baking powder

½ teaspoon baking soda

1 cup sugar

½ cup butter or margarine, softened

2 teaspoons grated lemon peel

1 teaspoon lemon juice

1 teaspoon cinnamon

2 eggs or equivalent amount of egg substitute

¾ cup canned poppy seed filling for cakes and pastry

¾ cup buttermilk

confectioners' sugar

◆ Grease the side and bottom of a bundt pan or spray with nonstick cooking spray.

◆ Sift the cake flour, baking powder and baking soda together.

◆ Beat the sugar, butter, lemon peel, lemon juice and cinnamon in a mixer bowl until creamy, scraping the bowl occasionally.

◆ Add the eggs 1 at a time, mixing well after each addition.

◆ Beat until light and fluffy, scraping the bowl occasionally.

◆ Combine the poppy seed filling and buttermilk in a bowl and mix well.

◆ Add the dry ingredients and poppy seed filling mixture alternately, mixing well after each addition.

◆ Spoon into the prepared pan and smooth top with the back of a spoon.

◆ Bake at 325 degrees for 1 hour.

◆ Cool in pan on a wire rack. Invert onto a serving platter.

◆ Dust with confectioners' sugar.

 Brown Sugar Pound Cake — Serves 16

For the Cake

3 cups flour

$^1/_2$ teaspoon salt

$^1/_2$ teaspoon baking powder

1 cup evaporated skim milk

$^1/_2$ teaspoon vanilla extract

1 cup butter or margarine, softened

1 cup vegetable shortening

1 (16-ounce) package light brown sugar

5 eggs

For the Confectioners' Sugar Frosting

$^1/_2$ cup margarine

1 cup packed brown sugar

3 cups confectioners' sugar

$^1/_4$ cup evaporated skim milk

1 teaspoon vanilla extract

- ◆ To prepare the cake, mix the flour, salt and baking powder in a bowl.

- ◆ Combine the evaporated skim milk and vanilla in a bowl and mix well.

- ◆ Beat the butter and shortening in a mixer bowl until creamy. Add the brown sugar gradually, beating until light and fluffy.

- ◆ Add the eggs 1 at a time, beating well after each addition.

- ◆ Add the dry ingredients alternately with the evaporated skim milk mixture, mixing well after each addition.

- ◆ Spoon the batter into a greased and floured 10-inch tube pan.

- ◆ Bake at 350 degrees for 1 hour.

- ◆ Cool in pan on a wire rack for 15 to 20 minutes. Invert onto wire rack to cook completely.

- ◆ To prepare the frosting, heat the margarine in a saucepan over medium heat until melted. Add the brown sugar.

- ◆ Cook until the brown sugar melts, stirring constantly. Remove from heat.

- ◆ Add the confectioners' sugar, evaporated skim milk and vanilla.

- ◆ Whisk until creamy and of a spreading consistency. Cool slightly.

- ◆ Spread over the cake.

# Rich Pound Cake

Serves 16

9 egg whites

3 cups sifted flour

1 teaspoon baking powder

1/2 teaspoon salt

1 cup sugar

9 egg yolks

2 cups butter or margarine, softened

1 cup sugar

2 teaspoons vanilla extract

- ◆ Let the egg whites stand at room temperature for 1 hour.

- ◆ Sift the flour, baking powder and salt together.

- ◆ Beat the egg whites in a mixer bowl at high speed until foamy. Add 1 cup sugar 1/4 cup at a time, beating well after each addition.

- ◆ Beat until soft peaks form. Spoon into a bowl.

- ◆ Beat the egg yolks, butter, 1 cup sugar and vanilla in the same mixer bowl at high speed until blended. Add the dry ingredients.

- ◆ Beat at low speed just until smooth.

- ◆ Add the egg white mixture gradually, beating at low speed just until blended.

- ◆ Spoon into a greased and floured 10-inch tube pan.

- ◆ Bake at 350 degrees for 1 hour or until a wooden pick inserted in the center comes out clean.

- ◆ Cool in pan on a wire rack for 15 minutes. Invert onto wire rack to cool completely.

 Sour Cream Pound Cake   Serves 16

3 cups flour
1/4 teaspoon baking soda
1/4 teaspoon salt
3 cups sugar
1 cup butter, softened
1 1/2 teaspoons vanilla extract
6 eggs
1 cup sour cream

◆ Sift the flour, baking soda and salt together.

◆ Beat the sugar and butter in a mixer bowl until creamy, scraping the bowl occasionally. Add the vanilla and mix well.

◆ Add the eggs 1 at a time, mixing well after each addition.

◆ Add the sour cream and dry ingredients alternately, mixing well after each addition.

◆ Beat for 5 minutes longer or until light and fluffy, scraping the bowl occasionally.

◆ Spoon into an oiled bundt pan.

◆ Bake at 325 degrees for 1 1/2 hours.

◆ Cool in pan on a wire rack for 15 minutes. Invert onto wire rack to cool completely.

 Rum Walnut Cake   *Serves 16*

For the Rum Sauce

1¼ cups sugar

1 cup sugar

⅓ cup rum

For the Cake

⅓ cup butter or margarine

6 egg whites

1 teaspoon salt

¼ teaspoon cream of tartar

¼ cup confectioners' sugar

6 egg yolks

1 cup sugar

1 teaspoon vanilla extract

1 teaspoon rum extract

1⅔ cups flour

1½ cups chopped walnuts

confectioners' sugar

- To prepare the sauce, combine the sugar and water in a saucepan and mix well.

- Simmer for 10 minutes, stirring occasionally.

- Let stand until cool. Stir in the rum.

- To prepare the cake, heat the butter in a saucepan until melted.

- Let stand until cool.

- Beat the egg whites, salt and cream of tartar in a mixer bowl until soft peaks form.

- Add ¼ cup confectioners' sugar gradually, beating constantly until stiff but not dry peaks form.

- Beat the egg yolks in a mixer bowl just until blended. Add the sugar and flavorings.

- Beat until thick and creamy, scraping the bowl occasionally.

- Sprinkle the flour over the egg whites. Pour the egg yolk mixture over the flour. Fold together until partially blended.

- Fold in the butter and walnuts just until blended. Spoon into a greased and floured bundt pan.

- Bake at 350 degrees for 45 minutes.

- Cool in pan on a wire rack for 10 minutes.

- Pierce the top of the cake with a wooden skewer. Drizzle with the Rum Sauce.

- Invert the cake onto a serving platter.

- Let stand until cool. Dust with confectioners' sugar.

Note:

Substitute Buttercream Frosting (page 142) for the Rum Sauce if desired.

Baker's Frosting

Makes 2 cups

½ cup vegetable shortening

½ cup margarine, softened

½ cup plus 2 tablespoons
confectioners' sugar

2 egg whites

1 (5-ounce) can (or less)
evaporated milk

1 teaspoon vanilla extract

◆ Beat the shortening, margarine and confectioners'
sugar in a mixer bowl until creamy. Add the
egg whites.

◆ Beat until blended. Add just the amount of
evaporated milk and the vanilla to have the
consistency of heavy whipped cream, beating
constantly at low speed until blended.

Raspberry Sauce

Makes 2 cups

2 (12-ounce) packages frozen
unsweetened raspberries,
thawed

½ cup sugar

2 tablespoons raspberry liqueur

◆ Combine the raspberries, sugar and liqueur in a food
processor container.

◆ Process until puréed.

◆ Strain into a bowl.

◆ Chill, covered, in the refrigerator.

Note:
May be prepared 1 day in advance and stored, covered,
in the refrigerator.

Desserts

 Cheesecake

Serves 16

1 recipe graham cracker crust

16 ounces cream cheese, softened

1 cup sugar

2 cups sour cream

2 tablespoons flour

1 tablespoon lemon juice

1 teaspoon vanilla extract

◆ Prepare the graham cracker crust. Press over the bottom and up the side of a springform pan.

◆ Bake using the recipe directions.

◆ Let stand until cool.

◆ Beat the cream cheese and sugar in a mixer bowl until creamy.

◆ Beat for 5 minutes, scraping the bowl occasionally.

◆ Add the sour cream, flour, lemon juice and vanilla, mixing well after each addition.

◆ Beat at high speed for 10 minutes, scraping the bowl occasionally. The longer the mixture is beaten the lighter the cheesecake.

◆ Spoon into the prepared pan.

◆ Bake at 350 degrees for 1 hour or until the center appears almost set. Cover with foil if the top begins to brown.

◆ Chill, covered, for 8 to 10 hours before serving.

Variation:
Top with sliced fresh fruit for a more elegant dessert.

 Apple Brandy Cheesecake

Serves 16

For the Cinnamon Crust

1¼ cups graham cracker crumbs

½ cup ground walnuts or pecans

1 teaspoon cinnamon

¼ cup melted margarine or
  butter, cooled

For the Cream Cheese Filling

32 ounces cream cheese,
  softened

1 cup sugar

1 cup applesauce

1 cup sour cream

½ cup whipping cream

4 eggs or equivalent amount of
  egg substitute

1 tablespoon cinnamon

1 teaspoon nutmeg

1 tablespoon vanilla extract

3 tablespoons apple brandy

¼ cup flour

For the Crumb Topping

¾ cup packed brown sugar

¾ cup flour

¼ cup melted butter or
  margarine

1 teaspoon cinnamon

½ teaspoon nutmeg

- To prepare the crust, combine the graham cracker crumbs, walnuts, cinnamon and margarine in a bowl and mix well.

- Press the crumb mixture over the bottom and 2 inches up the side of a springform pan sprayed with nonstick cooking spray.

- Bake at 350 degrees for 10 minutes.

- Let stand until cool.

- To prepare the filling, beat the cream cheese and sugar in a mixer bowl until smooth.

- Add the applesauce, sour cream, whipping cream, eggs, cinnamon, nutmeg, vanilla, apple brandy and flour in the order listed, mixing well after each addition.

- Beat at medium speed for 8 minutes, scraping the bowl occasionally.

- Spoon into the prepared springform pan.

- Bake at 350 degrees for 50 to 60 minutes or until the center appears almost set.

- To prepare the topping, combine the brown sugar, flour, butter, cinnamon and nutmeg in a bowl and mix well. Sprinkle over the top of the cheesecake.

- Bake at 350 degrees for 10 minutes or until light brown.

- Let stand until cool.

- Chill, covered, for 4 to 10 hours before serving.

 Lime Cheesecake   Serves 16

For the Gingersnap Crust

2 cups crushed gingersnaps

1/2 cup sugar

5 tablespoons melted margarine, cooled

For the Cream Cheese Filling

24 ounces cream cheese, softened

1 1/2 cups sugar

2 cups sour cream

2 extra-large egg whites, at room temperature, lightly beaten

3 tablespoons grated lime peel

1/4 cup fresh lime juice

3 tablespoons flour

For the Sour Cream Topping

1 cup sour cream

1/4 cup sugar

sliced fresh fruits

◆ To prepare the crust, combine the gingersnap crumbs, sugar and margarine in a bowl and mix well.

◆ Press the crumb mixture over the bottom and up the side of a springform pan sprayed with nonstick cooking spray.

◆ To prepare the filling, beat the cream cheese and sugar in a mixer bowl until smooth. Add the sour cream, egg whites, lime peel, lime juice and flour 1 ingredient at a time, mixing well after each addition.

◆ Beat at medium speed for 10 minutes, scraping the bowl occasionally.

◆ Spoon into the prepared springform pan.

◆ Bake at 350 degrees for 1 hour. The top should be light brown.

◆ Let stand until cool.

◆ Chill, covered, for 4 to 10 hours. The flavor is enhanced if chilled for 8 to 10 hours.

◆ To prepare the topping, beat the sour cream and sugar in a bowl until blended. Spread over the cooled layers.

◆ Top with sliced fresh fruits of your choice.

Oreo Cheesecake

Serves 16

For the Oreo Crust

1 1/2 cups Oreo cookie crumbs

1/4 cup melted margarine

For the Oreo Filling

2 pounds cream cheese, softened

1 1/4 cups sugar

4 eggs

2 egg whites

2 tablespoons flour

1 teaspoon vanilla extract

1/3 cup whipping cream

12 Oreos, ground

2 cups sour cream

1/4 cup sugar

1 teaspoon vanilla extract

For the Chocolate Topping

2 cups whipping cream

8 ounces semisweet chocolate

1 teaspoon vanilla extract

Oreo cookies

◆ To prepare the crust, combine the cookie crumbs and margarine in a bowl, stirring until crumbly. Press the crumb mixture over the bottom and 2 inches up the side of a 9-inch springform pan sprayed with nonstick cooking spray. Bake at 325 degrees for 8 minutes.

◆ To prepare the filling, beat the cream cheese and 1 1/4 cups sugar in a mixer bowl until smooth. Add the eggs 1 at a time, beating well after each addition.

◆ Whisk the egg whites in a bowl until frothy. Add to the cream cheese mixture and mix well. Add the flour and 1 teaspoon vanilla and mix until smooth. Add the whipping cream gradually, beating until blended.

◆ Spoon half the cream cheese mixture into the prepared pan. Sprinkle with the ground Oreos. Top with the remaining cream cheese mixture.

◆ Bake at 425 degrees for 15 minutes. Reduce the oven temperature to 225 degrees. Bake for 50 minutes. Remove from oven. Increase the oven temperature to 350 degrees.

◆ Mix the sour cream, 1/4 cup sugar and 1 teaspoon vanilla in a bowl. Spread over the hot cake. Bake for 10 minutes longer. Let stand until cool. Chill, covered, for 8 to 10 hours.

◆ To prepare the topping, combine the whipping cream, chocolate and vanilla in a saucepan. Cook over medium heat until the chocolate melts, stirring constantly. Remove from heat.

◆ Stir until the mixture is smooth and glossy. Pour over the chilled cheesecake, allowing the topping to drizzle down the side.

◆ Cut the Oreos into halves. Arrange the cookie halves around the top, allowing the edges of the cookies to touch. Chill, covered, until serving time.

Piña Colada Cheesecake

Serves 6 to 8

2 (14-ounce) cans sweetened
    condensed milk
¹/₂ cup cream of coconut
¹/₂ cup frozen concentrated lime
    juice
24 ounces light whipped
    topping
2 egg whites
¹/₂ cup sugar
2 cups flaked coconut
1 baked (8- or 9-inch) pie shell

◆ Combine the condensed milk, cream of coconut and lime juice in a bowl and mix well.

◆ Fold in the whipped topping.

◆ Beat the egg whites in a mixer bowl until frothy. Add the sugar gradually, beating constantly until moist and glossy. Fold into the coconut mixture.

◆ Fold in 1¹/₂ cups of the flaked coconut. Pour into the pie shell and mound.

◆ Sprinkle with the remaining ¹/₂ cup flaked coconut.

◆ Chill, covered, until serving time.

 Pumpkin Cheesecake   Serves 16

For the Gingersnap Crust

1¹/₂ cups pecans

2 tablespoons sugar

1 cup gingersnap crumbs

5 tablespoons melted unsalted
 butter

For the Pumpkin Filling

16 ounces cream cheese,
 softened

²/₃ cup packed brown sugar

1 cup canned solid-pack
 pumpkin

1 cup sour cream, at room
 temperature

3 eggs, at room temperature

1 tablespoon fresh lemon juice

1 teaspoon cinnamon

¹/₂ teaspoon ground cloves

¹/₂ teaspoon ginger

pecan halves

- To prepare the crust, process the pecans and sugar in a blender for 20 seconds or until finely ground.

- Combine the pecan mixture and gingersnap crumbs in a bowl and mix well. Stir in the butter.

- Press the crumb mixture over the bottom and up the side of a 10-inch springform pan sprayed with nonstick cooking spray.

- Bake at 325 degrees for 10 minutes.

- Let stand until cool.

- To prepare the filling, beat the cream cheese and brown sugar in a mixer bowl until blended. Stir in the pumpkin and sour cream.

- Add the eggs, lemon juice, cinnamon, cloves and ginger gradually, beating constantly until blended.

- Spoon into the prepared springform pan.

- Bake at 325 degrees for 45 minutes or until set.

- Let stand until cool. Top with the pecan halves.

- Chill, covered, for 8 to 10 hours.

 Bread Pudding

Serves 16

2 cups evaporated skim milk

1 cup light sour cream

1 cup whipping cream

8 eggs, beaten

6 tablespoons sugar

1 tablespoon nutmeg

1 tablespoon ginger

1 cup golden raisins

1 loaf butter bread, crusts trimmed, cubed

1 day-old coffee cake, cubed

honey

1/2 cup melted butter or margarine

3/4 cup packed brown sugar

◆ Combine the evaporated skim milk, sour cream, whipping cream, eggs, sugar, nutmeg and ginger in a bowl and mix well. Stir in the raisins.

◆ Add the bread cubes and coffee cake cubes and mix gently.

◆ Spread a thin layer of honey over the bottom of a 9x13-inch baking pan. Drizzle with the butter.

◆ Pour the bread mixture into the prepared pan. Sprinkle with brown sugar.

◆ Place the baking pan in a larger pan. Add water to the larger pan to measure 2 inches.

◆ Bake at 300 degrees for 45 to 60 minutes or until set.

 Raisin Rice Pudding

Serves 20

2 cups rice

milk

4 cups vanilla pudding or
    custard

2 cups raisins

1 cup milk

2 tablespoons cinnamon

2 tablespoons vanilla extract

3 tablespoons sugar

1 tablespoon cinnamon

- ◆ Cook the rice using package directions and substituting milk for the liquid.

- ◆ Let stand until cool.

- ◆ Combine the rice, pudding, raisins, 1 cup milk, 2 tablespoons cinnamon and vanilla in a bowl and mix well.

- ◆ Pour into a large 9x13-inch or larger roasting pan sprayed with nonstick cooking spray.

- ◆ Sprinkle the top with a mixture of the sugar and 1 tablespoon cinnamon.

- ◆ Bake at 350 degrees for 45 to 60 minutes or until set; do not overcook.

Chocolate Hazelnut Mousse

Serves 4

½ cup hazelnuts, toasted

1 tablespoon sugar

4 ounces bittersweet chocolate, chopped

3 egg yolks

2 tablespoons water

2 tablespoons brandy or rum

2 tablespoons sugar

3 egg whites

⅛ teaspoon salt

2 tablespoons sugar

3 tablespoons water

½ cup whipping cream, chilled

whipped cream

chopped toasted hazelnuts

- ◆ Process ½ cup hazelnuts and 1 tablespoon sugar in a food processor until the mixture form a paste.

- ◆ Place the chocolate in a small metal bowl. Set the bowl over simmering water in a saucepan. Stir until smooth. Remove the bowl from over the water.

- ◆ Whisk the egg yolks, 2 tablespoons water, brandy and 2 tablespoons sugar in a bowl until blended. Set the bowl over simmering water in a saucepan.

- ◆ Whisk constantly for 6 minutes or until thick ribbons form when the whisk is lifted out of the mixture.

- ◆ Cool slightly. Fold in the hazelnut paste and the chocolate.

- ◆ Beat the egg whites and salt in a mixer bowl until soft peaks form.

- ◆ Combine 2 tablespoons sugar and 3 tablespoons water in a small saucepan.

- ◆ Cook over medium heat until the sugar dissolves, stirring constantly. Increase the heat. Bring to a boil.

- ◆ Boil for 4 minutes, stirring frequently.

- ◆ Add the hot syrup to the egg whites gradually. Fold into the chocolate mixture in 2 batches.

- ◆ Beat the whipping cream in a mixer bowl until soft peaks form. Fold into the mousse.

- ◆ Spoon the mousse into 4 glasses.

- ◆ Chill for 1 hour or longer. Top with whipped cream and chopped toasted hazelnuts.

 Flourless Chocolate Torte

Serves 16

7 ounces bittersweet or
   semisweet chocolate, chopped
³/₄ cup unsalted butter
1¹/₃ cups sugar
4 eggs
1 teaspoon espresso powder or
   instant coffee powder
confectioners' sugar

◆ Coat the bottom and side of an 8-inch springform pan with butter; sprinkle with sugar. Wrap foil around the outside of the pan.

◆ Heat the chocolate and ³/₄ cup butter in a heavy saucepan over low heat until blended, stirring constantly.

◆ Whisk the sugar, eggs and espresso powder in a bowl until blended. Whisk in the chocolate mixture.

◆ Spoon into the prepared pan.

◆ Place the springform pan in a larger baking pan. Add hot water to reach halfway up the side of the springform pan.

◆ Bake at 325 degrees for 1¹/₂ hours or until a knife inserted in the center comes out clean. The cake will be approximately ¹/₂ inch high. Remove cake from water bath.

◆ Let stand until cool. Discard foil.

◆ Chill, covered, for 8 to 10 hours. Remove side of pan.

◆ Sprinkle top with confectioners' sugar. Cut into wedges.

Note:
Can be prepared 1 week in advance and stored, covered, in the refrigerator.

 Easy Strudel

Makes 1 dozen

2 cups flour

1 cup butter, softened

8 ounces cream cheese, softened

1/8 teaspoon salt

melted butter or margarine

1 (12-ounce) jar apricot or
   strawberry preserves

1 cup sugar

1 cup chopped nuts

1 cup golden raisins

1/4 cup cinnamon

confectioners' sugar

◆ Combine the flour, 1 cup butter, cream cheese and salt in a bowl and mix well. Shape into a ball.

◆ Chill, wrapped in waxed paper, in the refrigerator.

◆ Divide the pastry into 4 equal portions.

◆ Roll each portion into a rectangle on a lightly floured surface.

◆ Brush each rectangle with melted butter. Spread with the preserves.

◆ Sprinkle with the sugar, nuts, raisins and cinnamon.

◆ Roll as for a jelly roll. Pinch ends to seal.

◆ Place seam side down on a baking sheet. Brush with melted butter.

◆ Bake at 350 degrees for 20 to 25 minutes or until brown.

◆ Let stand until cool.

◆ Cut into 1-inch slices. Dust with confectioners' sugar.

 # Fudgy Brownies

Makes 16 bars

4 ounces unsweetened chocolate

¹/₂ cup butter or margarine

2 cups sugar

4 eggs or equivalent amount of
    egg substitute

¹/₂ cup unsweetened applesauce

1¹/₃ cups flour

1 teaspoon baking powder

2 teaspoons vanilla extract

1¹/₂ cups chopped nuts

◆ Combine the chocolate and butter in a
heavy saucepan.

◆ Cook over low heat until blended, stirring
frequently. Do not boil.

◆ Let stand until cool.

◆ Beat the sugar and eggs in a mixer bowl until pale
yellow. Stir in the applesauce. Add the chocolate
mixture and mix well.

◆ Mix the flour and baking powder in a bowl. Add to
the chocolate mixture gradually, mixing well after
each addition.

◆ Stir in the vanilla and nuts.

◆ Spoon into an 8x8-inch baking pan sprayed with
nonstick cooking spray.

◆ Bake at 350 degrees for 30 to 35 minutes.

◆ Let stand until cool. Cut into bars.

 Golden Brownies

Makes 16 bars

1 cup flour

¾ teaspoon baking powder

⅛ teaspoon salt

⅛ teaspoon baking soda

½ cup plus 2 tablespoons
   unsalted butter, softened

¾ cup packed light brown sugar

1 teaspoon vanilla extract

1 egg

1½ cups vanilla milk
   (white chocolate) chips

1 cup chopped pecans

◆ Combine the flour, baking powder, salt and baking soda in a bowl and mix well.

◆ Beat the butter, brown sugar and vanilla in a mixer bowl until light and fluffy, scraping the bowl occasionally. Add the egg.

◆ Beat until blended. Stir in the dry ingredients.

◆ Add the vanilla milk chips and pecans and mix well.

◆ Spoon into an 8x8-inch baking pan sprayed with nonstick cooking spray

◆ Bake at 350 degrees for 15 minutes or until golden brown.

◆ Let stand until cool. Cut into bars.

# Black Bottoms

Makes 3 dozen

8 ounces cream cheese, softened

¹/₃ cup sugar

1 egg, beaten

¹/₈ teaspoon salt

1 cup semisweet chocolate chips

1¹/₂ cups flour

1 cup sugar

¹/₂ cup baking cocoa

1 teaspoon baking soda

¹/₂ teaspoon salt

1 cup water

¹/₂ cup vegetable oil

1 tablespoon vinegar

1 teaspoon vanilla extract

◆ Beat the cream cheese, ¹/₃ cup sugar, egg and ¹/₈ teaspoon salt in a mixer bowl until blended, scraping the bowl occasionally. Stir in the chocolate chips.

◆ Sift the flour, 1 cup sugar, baking cocoa, baking soda and ¹/₂ teaspoon salt into a bowl and mix well.

◆ Mix the water, oil, vinegar and vanilla in a bowl. Stir into the dry ingredients.

◆ Fill muffin cups half full of the cocoa mixture. Top with the cream cheese mixture. Be careful not to fill the muffin cups too full.

◆ Bake at 350 degrees for 30 minutes.

Note:
Bake in miniature muffin cups at 350 degrees for 20 minutes.

Chocolate Chip and Everything Else Cookies

Makes 5 to 6 dozen

2 cups sifted flour

2 teaspoons baking soda

1 teaspoon baking powder

1 teaspoon cinnamon

1/2 teaspoon salt

1 cup butter or margarine, softened

1 cup packed brown sugar

1 cup sugar

1 tablespoon vanilla extract

2 eggs

2 cups rolled oats

1 cup golden raisins

1 cup chopped nuts

◆ Sift the flour, baking soda, baking powder, cinnamon and salt together.

◆ Beat the butter, brown sugar and sugar in a mixer bowl until creamy, scraping the bowl occasionally. Mix in the vanilla.

◆ Add the eggs 1 at a time, beating well after each addition.

◆ Add the dry ingredients gradually, beating constantly until blended.

◆ Stir in the oats, raisins and nuts.

◆ Drop by rounded tablespoonfuls onto a cookie sheet sprayed with nonstick cooking spray.

◆ Bake at 350 degrees for 15 to 18 minutes or until golden brown.

◆ Cool on cookie sheet for 2 minutes. Remove to a wire rack to cool completely.

Variation:

Substitute shredded coconut or chocolate chips for the nuts or use a combination of the nuts, coconut and chocolate chips.

White Chocolate Macadamia Nut Cookies

Makes 3 dozen

1 cup flour

³/₄ teaspoon baking powder

¹/₈ teaspoon salt

¹/₈ teaspoon baking soda

¹/₂ cup plus 2 tablespoons unsalted butter, softened

³/₄ cup packed light brown sugar

1 teaspoon vanilla extract

1 egg

1¹/₂ cups white chocolate chips

³/₄ cup coarsely chopped macadamia nuts

³/₄ cup coarsely chopped pecans

- ◆ Mix the flour, baking powder, salt and baking soda in a bowl.

- ◆ Beat the butter, brown sugar and vanilla in a mixer bowl until light and fluffy, scraping the bowl occasionally. Mix in the egg.

- ◆ Add the dry ingredients gradually, stirring until blended.

- ◆ Stir in the white chocolate chips, macadamia nuts and pecans.

- ◆ Drop by scant ¹/₄ cupfuls onto 2 greased heavy cookie sheets.

- ◆ Bake at 350 degrees for 15 minutes or until golden brown.

- ◆ Cool on cookie sheets for 2 minutes. Remove to a wire rack to cool completely.

Candy Bar Cookies

Makes 3 dozen

2 cups sugar

3/4 cup melted butter or
    margarine

4 eggs, lightly beaten

2 teaspoons vanilla extract

1¹/₂ cups flour

¹/₃ cup baking cocoa

¹/₂ teaspoon baking powder

¹/₂ teaspoon salt

4 (2-ounce) chocolate-coated
    caramel peanut nougat candy
    bars, coarsely chopped

3 (1.5-ounce) milk chocolate
    bars, finely chopped

- ◆ Combine the sugar, butter, eggs and vanilla in a bowl and mix well.

- ◆ Combine the flour, baking cocoa, baking powder and salt in a bowl and mix well. Stir into the sugar mixture.

- ◆ Fold in the nougat candy bars.

- ◆ Spoon into a greased and floured 9x13-inch baking pan. Sprinkle with the milk chocolate.

- ◆ Bake at 350 degrees for 30 to 35 minutes.

- ◆ Let stand until cool. Cut into squares.

 Oatmeal Cookies   Makes 4 dozen

1 cup packed brown sugar

1 cup sugar

$^1/_2$ cup butter, softened

$^1/_2$ cup margarine, softened

2 eggs

2$^1/_4$ cups flour

1 teaspoon baking soda

1 teaspoon vanilla extract

few drops of warm water

3 cups rolled oats

1 cup milk chocolate chips

1 cup chopped walnuts

◆ Beat the brown sugar, sugar, butter and margarine in a mixer bowl until creamy, scraping the bowl occasionally.

◆ Add the eggs, beating until blended.

◆ Add the flour, baking soda, vanilla and warm water and mix well. Stir in the oats, chocolate and walnuts.

◆ Drop by teaspoonfuls 2 inches apart on a nonstick cookie sheet.

◆ Bake at 360 degrees for 20 minutes.

◆ Cool on cookie sheet for 2 minutes. Remove to a wire rack to cool completely.

Rugelach

Makes 4 dozen

8 ounces cream cheese, softened

2 cups flour

1 cup butter, softened

2 tablespoons sugar

flour

1/2 cup melted butter or
   margarine

1 (12-ounce) jar apricot jam

1 cup finely chopped pecans

1 cup golden raisins

1 cup sugar

2 tablespoons cinnamon

confectioners' sugar

- ◆ Combine the cream cheese, 2 cups flour, 1 cup butter and 2 tablespoons sugar in a bowl and mix well.

- ◆ Divide the dough into 4 portions. Dust with flour.

- ◆ Shape each portion into a ball and wrap with waxed paper.

- ◆ Chill for 1 hour.

- ◆ Roll each ball into a 10x15-inch rectangle on a lightly floured surface. Brush with melted butter.

- ◆ Spread each rectangle to within 1 inch of the edges with jam.

- ◆ Combine the pecans, raisins, 1 cup sugar and cinnamon in a bowl and mix well. Sprinkle over the jam.

- ◆ Roll as for a jelly roll. Place seam side down on a baking sheet.

- ◆ Brush with melted butter.

- ◆ Bake at 375 degrees for 20 minutes or until golden brown.

- ◆ Cool just until warm.

- ◆ Cut into 1-inch slices. Dust with confectioners' sugar.

 Sugar Cookies

Makes 4 dozen

2¹/₄ cups sifted flour

1 teaspoon baking powder

1 teaspoon salt

1 cup sugar

³/₄ cup vegetable shortening

2 eggs

¹/₂ teaspoon vanilla or lemon
  extract

sugar to taste

- ◆ Sift the flour, baking powder and salt together.
- ◆ Beat 1 cup sugar, shortening, eggs and flavorings in a mixer bowl until creamy, scraping the bowl occasionally.
- ◆ Stir into the dry ingredients. Shape into a ball.
- ◆ Chill, covered, for 1 hour.
- ◆ Roll the dough ¹/₄ inch thick on a lightly floured surface. Cut with cookie cutter of choice.
- ◆ Place on a nonstick cookie sheet. Sprinkle with sugar to taste.
- ◆ Bake at 400 degrees for 6 to 8 minutes or until light brown.
- ◆ Cool on cookie sheet for 2 minutes. Remove to a wire rack to cool completely.

 Pumpkin Cookies   Makes 3 dozen

For the Cookies

2 cups flour

1 teaspoon baking powder

1 teaspoon baking soda

1 teaspoon cinnamon

1/2 teaspoon salt

1 cup vegetable shortening

1 cup sugar

1 cup pumpkin

1 egg

1 teaspoon vanilla extract

For the Brown Sugar Icing

1 cup packed brown sugar

1/2 cup butter or margarine

1/2 cup evaporated skim milk

2 cups confectioners' sugar

3/4 teaspoon vanilla extract

◆ To prepare the cookies, mix the flour, baking powder, baking soda, cinnamon and salt in a bowl.

◆ Beat the shortening, sugar, pumpkin, egg and vanilla in a mixer bowl until blended.

◆ Add the dry ingredients and mix well.

◆ Drop by teaspoonfuls 2 inches apart on a nonstick cookie sheet.

◆ Bake at 350 degrees for 10 minutes.

◆ To prepare the icing, combine the brown sugar, butter and evaporated skim milk in a saucepan. Bring to a boil.

◆ Boil for 2 minutes, stirring frequently. Remove from heat.

◆ Add the confectioners' sugar and vanilla gradually, beating until of a spreading consistency.

◆ Spread over the warm cookies.

 # Apple Pie

Serves 6 to 8

2 all ready pie pastries

1¼ cups sugar

2 tablespoons flour

1 teaspoon cinnamon

1 teaspoon nutmeg

⅛ teaspoon salt

6 cups thinly sliced peeled tart apples

2 teaspoons grated lemon peel

1 teaspoon lemon juice

2 tablespoons butter

1 egg yolk

1 tablespoon water

◆ Roll 1 of the pastries into an 11-inch circle on a lightly floured surface. Fit into a 9-inch pie plate.

◆ Chill in the refrigerator.

◆ Combine the sugar, flour, cinnamon, nutmeg and salt in a bowl and mix well. Add the apples, lemon peel and lemon juice and mix gently.

◆ Spoon the apple mixture into the chilled pastry-lined pie plate, mounding in the center. Dot with the butter.

◆ Roll the remaining pastry into an 11-inch circle on a lightly floured surface. Place over the apple mixture.

◆ Fold the edge of the top pastry under the bottom pastry and press. Crimp the edge. Make several decorative slits in the top.

◆ Beat the egg yolk and water in a bowl until blended. Brush over the top pastry.

◆ Bake at 425 degrees for 40 to 50 minutes or until golden brown.

◆ Serve warm.

Note:
May substitute 2 ready-made 9-inch pie shells for the all ready pie pastries.

 Apple Mincemeat Pie

Serves 6 to 8

1 recipe (2-crust) pie pastry
4 cups sliced peeled cooking
    apples
1 (28-ounce) jar mincemeat
2 tablespoons brandy
½ cup packed brown sugar
2 tablespoons grated lemon peel
2 teaspoons cornstarch
sugar to taste

◆ Roll half the pastry into a 12-inch circle on a lightly floured surface. Fit into a 9-inch pie plate.

◆ Place the apples in a heatproof colander or sieve. Set over simmering water in a large saucepan.

◆ Steam, covered, for 5 minutes or until the apples are tender but not mushy.

◆ Let stand until cool.

◆ Combine the mincemeat and brandy in a bowl and mix well. Spoon into the pastry-lined pie plate.

◆ Combine the apples, brown sugar, lemon peel and cornstarch in a bowl and mix well. Spoon over the mincemeat mixture.

◆ Roll the remaining pastry into a 12-inch circle on a lightly floured surface. Place over the apple filling.

◆ Fold the edge of the top pastry under the bottom pastry and seal. Flute the edge and cut vents.

◆ Sprinkle generously with sugar.

◆ Bake at 400 degrees for 40 to 50 minutes or until golden brown.

◆ Cool on a wire rack.

 # Berry Cheese Pie

Serves 6 to 8

8 ounces cream cheese, softened

1 cup sifted confectioners' sugar

1 teaspoon vanilla extract

1 cup whipped cream

1 (9-inch) graham cracker pie
   shell

1 (21-ounce) can cherry pie
   filling

◆ Beat the cream cheese and confectioners' sugar in a mixer bowl until smooth, scraping the bowl occasionally. Mix in the vanilla.

◆ Fold in the whipped cream.

◆ Spoon into the pie shell. Top with the cherry pie filling.

◆ Chill, covered, until serving time.

Note:
Substitute whipped topping for the whipped cream if time is of an essence. Use any berry pie filling as a topping.

Chocolate Cream Pie

Serves 6 to 8

3/4 cup sugar

1/3 cup cornstarch

2 ounces unsweetened chocolate, cut up

1/2 teaspoon salt

2 1/2 cups milk

3 egg yolks, lightly beaten

1/2 teaspoon vanilla extract

1 baked (9-inch) pie shell

- ◆ Combine the sugar, cornstarch, chocolate and salt in a double boiler.
- ◆ Add the milk gradually, stirring constantly.
- ◆ Cook over boiling water for 10 minutes or until thickened, stirring constantly.
- ◆ Cook, covered, for 10 minutes, stirring occasionally.
- ◆ Stir half the hot mixture into the egg yolks. Stir the egg yolks into the hot mixture.
- ◆ Cook over boiling water for 5 minutes, stirring occasionally. Remove from heat. Stir in the vanilla.
- ◆ Spoon into the pie shell
- ◆ Chill, covered, for 3 hours or longer.

 # Coconut Cream Pie

Serves 6 to 8

3/4 **cup sugar**

3 tablespoons cornstarch

1/2 **teaspoon salt**

2 1/2 **cups milk**

3 egg yolks, beaten

1 teaspoon vanilla

1 teaspoon butter or margarine

1 cup shredded coconut

1 baked (9-inch) pie shell

whipped cream or whipped topping

- ◆ Mix the sugar, cornstarch and salt in a double boiler. Stir in the milk.

- ◆ Cook over hot water over low heat for 15 minutes or until slightly thickened, stirring constantly.

- ◆ Stir a small amount of the hot mixture into the egg yolks. Stir the egg yolks into the hot mixture.

- ◆ Cook until thickened, stirring constantly. Remove from heat.

- ◆ Stir in the vanilla and butter.

- ◆ Set the pan in a bowl filled with ice water.

- ◆ Beat for 1 minute and cover.

- ◆ Beat 2 or more times or until of the consistency of French Cream. Be sure the water is kept ice cold.

- ◆ Stir in the coconut. Spoon into the pie shell.

- ◆ Top with whipped cream or whipped topping.

- ◆ Chill for 2 hours or longer before serving.

 # Lemon Pie

Serves 6 to 8

For the Pie

1 cup sugar

6 tablespoons cornstarch

1/8 teaspoon salt

2 cups water

3 egg yolks, beaten

1/3 cup lemon juice

3 tablespoons butter or
    margarine

3 tablespoons grated lemon peel

1 baked (9-inch) pie shell

For the Meringue

3 egg whites

1/4 teaspoon cream of tartar

6 tablespoons sugar

3/4 teaspoon vanilla extract

◆ To prepare the pie, combine the sugar, cornstarch and salt in a heavy saucepan and mix well. Stir in the water.

◆ Cook over medium-high heat for 8 minutes or until thickened, stirring constantly.

◆ Stir a small amount of the hot mixture into the egg yolks. Stir the egg yolks into the hot mixture.

◆ Cook for 3 minutes, stirring constantly. Remove from heat.

◆ Stir in the lemon juice, butter and lemon peel.

◆ Spoon into the pie shell.

◆ To prepare the meringue, beat the egg whites in a mixer bowl until frothy. Add the cream of tartar.

◆ Beat until mixed.

◆ Add the sugar and vanilla gradually, beating constantly until stiff peaks form.

◆ Mound over the filling, sealing to the edge and forming peaks with the side of a spatula.

◆ Bake at 300 degrees for 20 minutes or until light brown.

 # Southern Pecan Pie

Serves 6 to 8

4 eggs

1 cup light corn syrup

¹/₂ cup sugar

¹/₂ cup packed light brown sugar

1 tablespoon cornstarch

1 teaspoon vanilla extract

¹/₄ teaspoon salt

¹/₄ cup melted butter or
  margarine

2 cups pecan halves

1 (unbaked) 9-inch pie shell,
  chilled

whipped cream

◆ Beat the eggs in a bowl with a rotary beater.

◆ Add the corn syrup, sugar, brown sugar, cornstarch,
  vanilla and salt, beating until blended.

◆ Stir in the butter and pecans. Spoon into the
  pie shell.

◆ Bake at 350 degrees for 50 to 60 minutes or until the
  filling is firm in the center.

◆ Remove to a wire rack to cool. Chill slightly
  before serving.

◆ Top each serving with whipped cream.

Pumpkin Pecan Pie

Serves 6 to 8

3/4 **cup finely chopped pecans**

1/4 **cup sugar**

1 **(unbaked) 9-inch pie shell**

2 **eggs**

1 **(16-ounce) can pumpkin**

3/4 **cup packed brown sugar**

1 **teaspoon cinnamon**

1 **teaspoon ginger**

1 **teaspoon nutmeg**

1/2 **teaspoon ground cloves**

1/2 **teaspoon salt**

1 **(12-ounce) can evaporated skim milk**

1/2 **cup coarsely chopped pecans**

1/2 **cup packed brown sugar**

2 **tablespoons butter or margarine, softened**

◆ Mix 3/4 cup pecans and sugar in a bowl. Spread over the bottom of the pie shell.

◆ Beat the eggs lightly in a bowl. Add the pumpkin, 3/4 cup brown sugar, cinnamon, ginger, nutmeg, cloves and salt and mix well.

◆ Stir in the evaporated skim milk. Spoon into the prepared pie shell.

◆ Bake at 425 degrees for 15 minutes. Reduce the oven temperature to 375 degrees.

◆ Bake for 30 minutes longer or until a thin-bladed knife inserted 1 inch from the edge comes out clean.

◆ Remove to a wire rack to cool.

◆ Combine 1/2 cup pecans, 1/2 cup brown sugar and butter in a bowl and mix well. Sprinkle over cooled pie.

◆ Broil for 2 to 3 minutes or until brown and bubbly. Watch carefully, as the sugar will brown quickly.

◆ Remove to a wire rack to cool.

Old-Fashioned Pumpkin Pie

Serves 6 to 8

3 eggs
1 (16-ounce) can pumpkin
$1/2$ cup packed light brown sugar
$1/2$ cup sugar
$1^1/2$ teaspoons cinnamon
1 teaspoon ginger
1 teaspoon nutmeg
$1/2$ teaspoon ground cloves
$1/2$ teaspoon salt
$3/4$ cup evaporated skim milk
$1/2$ cup whipping cream
1 (unbaked) 9-inch pie shell

◆ Beat the eggs lightly in a bowl. Add the pumpkin, brown sugar, sugar, cinnamon, ginger, nutmeg, cloves and salt, beating until blended.

◆ Add the evaporated skim milk and whipping cream gradually and mix well.

◆ Spoon into the pie shell.

◆ Bake at 350 degrees for 50 to 60 minutes or until a knife inserted in the center comes out clean.

◆ Remove to a wire rack to cool.

Note:
May use a mixture of cream substitute and 1 tablespoon flour for the whipping cream.

 Snickers Bar Pie   Serves 6 to 8

1 (unbaked) 10-inch deep-dish
   pie shell

5 (2-ounce) Snickers

24 ounces cream cheese,
   softened

1 cup sugar

2 eggs

2 egg whites, beaten

1 cup light sour cream

1/2 cup peanut butter

3 tablespoons whipping cream
   (optional)

2/3 cup chocolate chips

2/3 cup chopped nuts

1 jar fat-free caramel sauce

- Bake the pie shell at 450 degrees for 5 to 7 minutes
  or until light brown.

- Let stand until cool. Reduce oven temperature to
  325 degrees.

- Cut the candy bars lengthwise into halves. Cut the
  halves into 1/4-inch pieces.

- Arrange the candy pieces over the bottom of the
  baked layer.

- Beat the cream cheese and sugar in a mixer bowl
  until creamy, scraping the bowl occasionally.

- Add the eggs 1 at a time, beating well after each
  addition. Beat in the egg whites.

- Add the sour cream and peanut butter, beating until
  smooth. Spoon over the candy pieces.

- Bake at 325 degrees for 30 to 40 minutes or until the
  center is set.

- Let stand until cool.

- Heat the whipping cream in a saucepan until very
  warm; do not boil. Remove from heat.

- Add the chocolate chips, stirring until smooth.
  Spoon over the pie.

- Chill for 2 to 3 hours or until set.

- Arrange the nuts in a 1 1/2-inch border around the
  edge of the pie. Spoon the caramel sauce over top of
  the pie, ending at the nut border.

- Chill, covered, until serving time.

 Strawberry Chocolate Tart

Serves 10 to 12

$^1/_4$ cup sugar

1$^1/_3$ cups unbleached flour

$^1/_2$ cup margarine, chilled, cut into pieces

2 egg whites, beaten

2 to 4 tablespoons cold water

1 teaspoon vanilla extract

1$^1/_2$ cups milk chocolate chips

2 quarts strawberries

1 large jar strawberry preserves

◆ Process the sugar in a food processor for 20 seconds. Add the flour and margarine.

◆ Pulse until the mixture resembles cornmeal.

◆ Mix the egg whites, cold water and vanilla in a bowl. Add to the processor gradually, processing constantly until the mixture forms a ball.

◆ Chill, wrapped in plastic wrap, for 1 hour.

◆ Roll the dough on a lightly floured surface to fit a 10-inch tart pan; roll dough 1$^1/_2$ inches larger than needed to fit 10-inch pan.

◆ Fit into the tart pan, folding the excess pastry under to form a rim and making the side thicker than the bottom.

◆ Line with waxed paper or foil. Place dried beans or pie weights over the bottom.

◆ Bake at 425 degrees for 10 minutes. Remove the beans and waxed paper.

◆ Bake until the edge is brown. Sprinkle with the chocolate chips.

◆ Let stand until the chocolate melts. Spread evenly over the bottom.

◆ Let stand until cool. Arrange the whole strawberries pointed end up in the shell.

◆ Heat the preserves in a saucepan just until warm. Spoon evenly over the strawberries.

◆ Chill, covered, until serving time.

# Lemon Macaroon Tartlets

Makes 1 dozen

For the Lemon Filling

2 cups sugar

2 tablespoons cornstarch

$^1\!/_2$ cup fresh lemon juice
(about 3 lemons)

$^1\!/_4$ cup butter

4 eggs, beaten

2 egg yolks, beaten

Grated peel of 1 lemon

For the Tart Shells

2 cups flaked coconut

$^1\!/_2$ cup sugar

$^1\!/_3$ cup flour

2 egg whites, beaten

1 teaspoon vanilla extract

- ◆ To prepare the filling, combine the sugar and cornstarch in a saucepan and mix well.

- ◆ Stir in the lemon juice, butter, eggs, egg yolks and lemon peel.

- ◆ Cook over low heat for 10 minutes or until thickened, stirring constantly.

- ◆ Let stand until cool.

- ◆ To prepare the shells, combine the coconut, sugar, flour, egg whites and vanilla in a bowl and mix well.

- ◆ Press the coconut mixture over the bottom and up the sides of the muffin cups. Spoon the filling into the prepared muffin cups.

- ◆ Bake at 400 degrees for 15 minutes or until the edges are brown.

- ◆ Cool in muffin cups for 2 minutes. Remove to a wire rack to cool completely.

 Basic Pie Crust

Makes 1 pie pastry

1¼ **cups sifted flour**
½ **cup margarine, chilled**
3 to 6 tablespoons ice water
1 teaspoon white vinegar

◆ Measure the flour into a food processor container.

◆ Cut the margarine into teaspoon-size portions. Add to the flour.

◆ Pulse until the mixture resembles cornmeal.

◆ Add the ice water and vinegar gradually, processing constantly until the mixture is moist and adheres. Shape into a ball.

◆ Chill, wrapped in plastic wrap, for 1 hour.

◆ Roll the dough ⅛ inch thick on a lightly floured surface 1½ inches larger than the pie plate.

◆ Fit the pastry into the pie plate. Trim, leaving a 1-inch overhang.

◆ Fold the excess pastry under. Press the outside edge with the tines of a fork or flute with your thumbs.

◆ Prick the bottom and side of the pie shell with a fork or line with dried beans or pie weights.

◆ Bake at 425 degrees for 10 minutes.

 Herbs

Use fresh whole herbs when possible. When fresh herbs are not available, use whole dried herbs that can be crushed just while adding. Store herbs in airtight containers away from the heat of the stove. Fresh herbs may be layered between paper towels and dried in the microwave on HIGH for 2 minutes or until dry.

- **Basil:** Can be chopped and added to cold poultry salads. If the recipe calls for tomatoes or tomato sauce, add a touch of basil to bring out a rich flavor.

- **Bay leaf:** The basis of many French seasonings. It is added to soups, stews, marinades and stuffings.

- **Bouquet garni:** A bundle of parsley, thyme and bay leaves tied together and added to stews, soups or sauces. Other herbs and spices may be added to the basic herbs.

- **Chervil:** One of the traditional fines herbs used in French cooking. (The others are tarragon, parsley and chives.) It is good in omelets and soups.

- **Chives:** Available fresh, dried or frozen, it can be substituted for raw onion or shallot in nearly any recipe.

- **Garlic:** One of the oldest herbs in the world, it must be carefully handled. For best results, press or crush the garlic clove.

- **Marjoram:** An aromatic herb of the mint family, it is good in soups, sauces, stuffings and stews.

- **Mint:** Use fresh, dried or ground with vegetables, desserts, fruits, jelly, lamb or tea. Fresh sprigs of mint make attractive aromatic garnishes.

- **Oregano:** A staple, savory herb in Italian, Spanish, Greek and Mexican cuisines. It is very good in dishes with a tomato foundation, especially in combination with basil.

- **Parsley:** Use this mild herb as fresh sprigs or dried flakes to flavor or garnish almost any dish.

- **Rosemary:** This pungent herb is especially good in poultry and fish dishes and in such accompaniments as stuffings.

- **Saffron:** Use this deep orange herb, made from the dried stamens of a crocus, sparingly in poultry, seafood and rice dishes.

- **Sage:** This herb is a perennial favorite with all kinds of poultry and stuffings.

- **Tarragon:** One of the fines herbs. Goes well with all poultry dishes whether hot or cold.

- **Thyme:** Usually used in combination with bay leaf in soups, stews and sauces.

 Index

FreshFields

3809 Crestside Road
Birmingham, Alabama 35223
Fax (205) 967-8073

Please send me _____ copies of *FreshFields* @ $19.95 each $ _____
add postage and handling @ $ 3.00 each $ _____
Alabama residents add sales tax @ $ 1.60 each $ _____
Total $ _____

❏ Check ❏ MasterCard ❏ VISA Card Number _____

Expiration Date _____ Signature _____

Name _____ Phone _____

Address _____

City _____ State _____ Zip _____

Please make checks payable to Bagatelle.

- -

FreshFields

3809 Crestside Road
Birmingham, Alabama 35223
Fax (205) 967-8073

Please send me _____ copies of *FreshFields* @ $19.95 each $ _____
add postage and handling @ $ 3.00 each $ _____
Alabama residents add sales tax @ $ 1.60 each $ _____
Total $ _____

❏ Check ❏ MasterCard ❏ VISA Card Number _____

Expiration Date _____ Signature _____

Name _____ Phone _____

Address _____

City _____ State _____ Zip _____

Please make checks payable to Bagatelle.

- -

Photocopies Accepted